10/89

BOOK SOCIETY

GRAHAM WATSON

BOOK SOCIETY

ATHENEUM   NEW YORK   1980

FOR DOROTHY, OF COURSE

FOREWORD

I F I am accused of name-dropping in this book I plead guilty. Even a partial autobiography is an exercise in egoism and this one is no exception, but it would not have been written had it not been the case that, through the accident of my trade, my life has been spent, to a large degree, in the presence of the well-known. Their personalities and activities are of continuing and legitimate interest and it is of them that I principally write. There have been a number of books written about book-trade politics and economics. This is not another one. Nor have I written in any detail about the day to day activities of literary agency. The reader who wishes to discover the earnings of a best-selling author, or the likely financial return from disposing of Swedish volume rights in a first novel will be disappointed. I hope that I have preserved the professional confidences of my clients. The book trade in which I have earned my living for forty-four years has changed beyond recognition. I have enjoyed recapturing a little of the savour of the past and if I can share that enjoyment with a few readers I shall be satisfied.

I have never kept a diary nor any records. Occasionally I have saved an odd letter or two which seemed of interest but this book has been written from memory. I am only too conscious that there may be mistakes of fact in it, but there is nothing which I know to be untrue. My life has been spent, on the whole, in the company of likeable people. Only exceptionally have I written about those I disliked. My aim is to give pleasure, not to settle old scores.

7

There will not, I fear, be much of interest for those who are not attracted by the essentially parochial, but nevertheless fascinating, affairs of the book trade in which the principal parts are played by authors, without whom there would be no book trade. I thought earnestly about the inclusion of the chapter on the war, which has scant bearing on the main theme. But it would seem absurd for someone of my generation to omit from even a partially autobiographical book six such traumatic years.

Lamb House, Rye.

BOOK SOCIETY

CHAPTER ONE

MANY readers, amongst whom I number myself, tend to skip the first three chapters of an autobiography, so that they encounter the author for the first time as, in the words of my father, Angus, occasionally wont to echo the Victorian moralists, 'he starts his voyage across the sea of life'. Not for them those harrowing tales of potty-training in the nursery. Not for them the recitals of frequent whippings in a private school. Not for them those tedious explorations along the branches of the family tree to establish the identity of boring Uncle Freddie, third cousin of Auntie Millie who, it will be remembered, married Sarah at the time of the Industrial Revolution.

This book has none of that. But it would be quite absurd for me to proceed directly to my adult activities without first introducing Angus who plays, from time to time, an important part in the events which follow.

Angus was born at Ryton-on-Tyne, seven miles up-river from Newcastle, in 1874. I still find it slightly disconcerting that the lives of the two of us span more than a century. Ryton, now a mining community and dormitory town of Newcastle, was then a small village grouped round the church on the village green. Life in the community centred round the school, which Angus attended, and the established and nonconformist churches which split social life between the classes. Angus, brought up a Congregationalist by parents, both of whom numbered a succession of ministers and preachers among their Scottish forebears, retained a devout faith throughout a life in which religion was to play a crucial role. When he was elected the Chairman of the

9

Congregational Union, only the third layman to be accorded that distinction, he valued it far above the other honours which came his way.

Angus's father was a fire-clay manufacturer producing such articles as pipes, bricks and tiling. His was a modest but reasonably prosperous business, employing a small workforce. On one occasion one of the workmen returned from lunch having consumed more than was wise of the gin which could then be bought for a penny a nip. My grandfather lectured the man and sacked him.

'One law for the rich and one for the poor,' said the man. 'You drink your wine and whisky and no one says a word. I have a drop too much gin and I get the sack.'

'You're quite right,' said my grandfather. 'We'll both sign the temperance pledge and you can keep your job.'

That night a small ceremony took place in the house at Ryton. My grandfather and grandmother collected all the bottles in the house and took them into the kitchen. The corks were pulled and, in the presence of the three children, the contents were ceremoniously poured down the sink. The children were then asked to sign the pledge and, for the remainder of his life, Angus remained a total abstainer. He was later to explain that this somewhat draconian decision was made because, in the days when he had been a commercial traveller on the road, it was always the practice to seal an order with a drink and he could see that his future posed the choice between total abstinence and total drunkenness. Whether or not this is true, he always maintained a strongly moralistic view about drinking.

His decision was later to produce certain tensions in the family when gin was no longer a penny a measure and the risks of alcoholism did not appear to loom so large. I remember a holiday spent in Maloja, a village on the border between Switzerland and Italy. Angus became friendly with a Dr Workman, a Methodist minister of unblemished character, and the two of them frequently went off on foot on day-long excursions. One such excursion took them into Italy and, the day being hot, they sat in an inviting café in the square of a village. The proprietor of the café approached for their order and doubtless quickly summed up the two Englishmen. Dr Workman, who claimed he spoke Italian, ordered two lemonades and the man departed, soon to return with a large bottle, the neck of which was wrapped in silver foil. Angus looked at it suspiciously. 'Ask him what it is.' Workman came out with some further elementary Italian. The man responded. 'He says it's a non-alcoholic wine made from gooseberries,' Dr Workman reported. They drank down the bottle. It tasted delicious. Later they turned up at the hotel, suspiciously exuberant, extolling the virtues of this new beverage. 'We'll have a bottle for dinner,' said Angus. 'It's called Asti-Spumante and the man in the café assured me it is non-alcoholic.' We drank it nightly, and with relish, for the rest of our holiday and although I think it dawned on Angus, eventually, that there was a difference between Italian-type champagne and temperance fizzy drinks, he had passed the point beyond which it could ever be publicly admitted. From then on Asti-Spumante was rated in our family as a temperance drink.

Angus left school at the age of fifteen. His father was then seventy, a great deal older than his mother who had been in poor health for some years. Two of Angus's sisters were at school in Germany and Switzerland – my grandmother was a feminist before her time – and the family finances, such as they were, were seriously diminishing. Although it had been Angus's ambition to go to university on the way to qualifying as a doctor, it became clear to him that he would very shortly have to fulfil the role of family provider. He left school one day without informing his father, applied for five jobs, all at five shillings a week, and was offered all five of them. Without much thought, he started the following week in the office of a grain and provision importer, a job which shortly led to an introduction to the man who was to play a leading role in what was to follow.

Hector Macdonald was a buying agent in the grocery trade and, as such, represented a widely disparate assortment of goods ranging from beef extract to Harris tweeds. Although Angus was originally hired as a book-keeper it was not long before he was out on the road selling the goods that the firm carried. It was on one of these occasions that he was shown by a grocer a new line in canned goods. It was a tin labelled 'Norwegian Sardines' and contained some small fish crudely packed in oil. Apart from their size there were two other features which distinguished them from sardines packed in France and Portugal which then accounted for the greater part of the world's consumption. They were free from bones and scales and they had a delicate flavour due to the curing process.

Macdonald and Angus were both attracted by this novel product and discussed the possibility of trying to acquire the English agency. A few days later Angus was on his way across the North Sea to make the first of many visits to Norway. Macdonald's parting instruction was, 'Make a big impression on a small expenditure.' That first visit resulted in a contract for the importation of a thousand cases of sardines in exchange for the sole agency in Great Britain. Within three months this order was increased to five thousand cases, and for the next three years the business continued to develop at a similar rate.

What would have come from a continuing association between Macdonald and Angus is a matter for speculation. Some years later Macdonald offered to sell Angus the business for four thousand pounds but by then the wheel had turned another circle and he was working as a traveller for W. H. Lever who was to make a fortune in soap and margarine. Later Lever was also to play an important part in Angus's life. Angus was soon making his mark in this rapidly growing organization and it was not long before he was summoned to Port Sunlight, the head office, where he was asked to lead a selling team to explore the potential market in America.

These were heady days for Angus. He was stimulated by America, he knew his abilities were being noticed at Port Sunlight, he was engaged to be married when he returned to England at the end of the agreed period of nine months, his future seemed assured. It was, therefore, with some confidence that he answered a further order to meet Lever in Toronto.

'I'm establishing a soapery in San Francisco,' said Lever. 'I want you to run it. The salary is fifteen hundred pounds and a share of the profits. Take a trip home to see your fiancée and when you've both agreed to my proposal, cable me from Liverpool "Acception".'

'And supposing I refuse?' said Angus.

'You won't,' said Lever, 'but then you cable "Rejection".'

Angus returned to England to discover that this was, indeed, the parting of the ways. In America he had an assured future in a country he liked. At home he found a letter from the Norwegian Canners offering him the management of their business. He saw Macdonald who had no objection to the suggestion. He had saved one thousand pounds and a friend, Henry Saint, had already offered him a further thousand pounds as an investment at the time when he was considering the purchase of Macdonald's agency. The offer, with Saint to be a sleeping partner, remained open. Angus cabled Lever 'Rejection' and in 1901 the firm of Angus Watson and Company was inaugurated. It consisted of a typist and an office boy, and the proprietor drew a salary of one hundred and fifty pounds per annum.

However, Angus was not to remain on that salary for long. He had a product the public appeared to want and he knew how to sell it. Before too many years were to pass the initial order for a thousand cases had grown into an annual sale of one hundred million tins. It was not altogether surprising, therefore, that before long this new enterprise attracted the attention of the French and Portuguese canners. One day, some six years after the inauguration of his business, Angus received a visit from a Frenchman. Without any preliminaries he announced the purpose of his visit. 'You have become a danger to the interests of the French sardine industry,' he said, 'and I am authorized to offer you £100,000 for your business.' Angus, gratified though he was at such a proposal, had no qualms about refusing it.

'Very well,' said the Frenchman. 'I suppose you know your business best, but I fear you may come to regret your decision.'

Shortly after this visit, Angus Watson and Co. were summoned to the Guildhall to answer a charge under the Merchandise Marks Act that they were applying the term 'sardine' to a product which could not properly be so described. This was the beginning of a case of Gilbertian hilarity which dragged through four courts, enriched the lawyers engaged and finally resulted in a finding for the French. By then the learned judges had come to the conclusion that the Norwegian brisling, whilst without doubt a member of the *Clupeoid* family, was a *Clupeoid sprattus*, whereas the sardine was a *Clupeoid pilcardus*. On such an issue is justice poised.

One side effect of the prolonged legal actions was that sales of brisling, now marketed under the trade name 'Skippers', increased as a result of the ensuing publicity. Another outcome was that Angus was made a Knight of St Olaf, a distinguished Norwegian honour which carried with it, by custom, an English baronetcy which he was offered and refused.

On which subject I might, perhaps, digress. As a Liberal, whose cause he actively espoused, he was once asked by a minion of Lloyd George whether he would like to purchase a peerage. Out of curiosity Angus asked the price. 'Ten thousand for a knighthood, twenty thousand for a peerage,' he was told.

Five years later, when Lloyd George's reputation was even further tarnished, and the party funds in further need of replenishment, Angus was again sounded out about a title. 'And what did you say it would cost me?' 'Twenty thousand for a knighthood, thirty thousand for a peerage,' he was told. 'But,' said Angus, 'five years ago the cost was ten thousand and twenty thousand.'

'Yes,' said Lloyd George's emissary, 'but since then the value of money has depreciated.'

'Yes,' said Angus, 'and so has the value of your honours.'

By the time the sardine litigation had meandered up to the House of Lords, war with Germany was in progress. Angus, too old to serve, was attached to the Ministry of Food where part of his duties concerned the purchase of canned goods, ostensibly through his own business although, in fact, on behalf of the government. This was thought to ensure that the prices paid would be reasonable and commercial. Although, of course, this arrangement meant that he had full financial backing from the Treasury, it also meant that his own business was permanently carrying an overdraft of some millions of pounds. Even with the coming of peace it was obvious to Angus that the firm was grossly under-capitalized. One day he happened by chance to be passing the offices of Lever Brothers and, although he had not seen his old employer, now Lord Leverhulme, for some years, on the spur of the moment he asked for an appointment. This meeting was to result in his obtaining the capital he required. The cost was the transfer of half the shares into the hands of Lord Leverhulme. It was an arrangement which worked well during Leverhulme's life time. But on his death Angus found the shares had passed, unknown to him, into the hands of Lever Brothers. This resulted in a relationship which, from the beginning, Angus knew, was not likely to work. On one side was a huge, impersonal con-glomerate. On the other, a personally owned business run on a basis of staff welfare, profit-sharing, and an employer-employee relationship which, a commonplace today, was then difficult to meld with a huge organization consisting of many subsidiary firms. In 1928 Angus, still only fifty-four, sold his remaining shares to Lever Brothers and left the firm he had so successfully created. With some of the money from the sale, he set up, in their own business, some half dozen of his executives who felt that they, too, must resign.

It was, I suppose, about this time that I, then aged fifteen, first got to know Angus. During the early years of my childhood, I had felt a little daunted by a figure whose business and other interests had left him little time for family affairs. His involvement in the Congregational Church, the keystone of his own life, was a divisive influence amongst his four children. I still recall with a chill those Sunday mornings in Newcastle. Between our large suburban house and the church of St James's lay a two-mile walk down a dreary, tram-lined road. At ten o'clock, promptly, the gong would sound and there was Angus standing impatiently in the hall in his blue overcoat and black velour hat. We filed gloomily along the endless-seeming pavements to arrive finally at St James's, always at least a quarter of an hour before the service was due to start and wondering how we would survive the next hour and a half without the Mint Imperials which my mother always passed down the pew to keep us quiet during the sermon.

One of the ministers was a Dr Jowett, a formidable preacher, whose sermons were famous for their length. On one occasion he was invited to preach in a small country church. He is reputed to have replied, briefly, on a postcard, 'Can an eagle sit on a sparrow's nest?'

St James's was to become the centre of a Sunday afternoon Forum run by Angus and to it came many well-known speakers, many of whom stayed the weekend with us. Angus always advised them in his invitation that we were a temperance house and many, I suspect, made provision for their several needs in the quiet of their bedrooms. G. K. Chesterton, however, had obviously ignored the warning. When he was refused a drink his face purpled. 'What!' he roared. 'Nothing for your guests to drink? Take me at once to the nearest hotel.'

As a matter of fact the St James's Forum, designed to enliven, with a talk on current affairs, a provincial Sunday afternoon before the inception of television, was for years a popular and well-supported feature in Newcastle. It also brought us children into contact with many distinguished public figures who accepted Angus's hospitality, dry or otherwise.

Religion, or Angus's version of it, later followed us to our country house in Rothbury, a village in the foothills of the Cheviots. There, every Sunday night, we had family prayers. Our chauffeur, Bewick, was an ex-jockey who used to whistle through his teeth as he groomed the cars. Bewick became the self-appointed convener of the staff for the Sunday evening worship. As the family sat waiting in the sitting room, we could hear in the distant kitchen the cook, maids and gardeners being marshalled by Bewick into orderly ranks and then marched down the corridor to where we sat waiting for them. It was fatal on these occasions to catch anyone's eye. Our local rector, Canon Rees, was a great eccentric of daunting intellectual attainment, who lived across the road in a vast rectory, once a Pele Tower, which Angus subsequently bought for the City of Newcastle as a home for deprived children. He arrived one night unannounced to discover the serried ranks on their knees in a circle round the sitting room. He surveyed us in some astonishment. 'Good heavens,' he said. 'May I join you?'

Canon Rees became a close friend of Angus who, no doubt attracted by sermons well above the heads of almost all the other members of the congregation, abandoned his local Congregational church, doubtless to the dismay of the top brass of the Congregational Union had they ever been informed of the desertion of an erstwhile chairman. However, if Angus, at least in Rothbury, preferred the Anglican services to those of his own church, he was not prepared publicly to make more concessions than were necessary to the opposition. As the Creed was intoned, his personal version rang through the nave in ringing tones: ' . . . and was incarnate by the Holy Spirit of the Mother Mary . . . ' It was a well-matched contest with Canon Rees.

But if religion was the leading force in Angus's life, he had many other interests, in some of which I was able to participate. One was a passion for walking in the Lake District where he always spent at least two holidays each year. On some of these holidays I used to accompany him. That I should have wanted to do so is surprising since my early years had been spent at a preparatory school in Windermere which I disliked as heartily as I was later to dislike Repton. However, there is a magic about the Lake District which transcends even a small boy's unhappiness. But my companions, for anyone of my age group, seem in retrospect a trifle bizarre.

Apart from Angus, the group always consisted of Harry Saint, then in his early seventies, and Jack Steele, a contemporary who was a successful businessman but mainly known for his reputation as a practical joker. His party piece was to walk up and down outside whatever hotel we had selected for lunch, cap in hand, singing Tyneside ballads in a corncrake baritone. Looking back I regret my embarrassment. On the face of it, this was unlikely society for a boy in his early teens, but I enjoyed their talk and all three men shed their normal serious mien and behaved like liberated schoolboys. None of their wives ever accompanied them on these excursions. As a rule the plan was to make day trips over the hills, starting from either Ullswater or Grasmere and we were met in the evening at some agreed rendezvous by Bewick with the car.

Angus's sense of direction was notoriously erratic, but he always managed to persuade the other two that he was right. On one occasion we came to a signpost late in the afternoon when we were all feeling a little tired, which said, Elter Water 5 miles, Rydal Water 3 miles. A heated argument ensued as to which was the right road to take. 'We should go to Rydal Water,' said Saint and Steele. 'No, no,' said Angus, 'I *know* we have to go to Elter Water.' We walked, inevitably, towards Elter Water. After forty minutes we arrived at another sign which read, Elter Water 5 miles, Skelwith Bridge 3 miles. 'Well,' said Steele, 'if we *should* be going to Elter Water, at least we're not losing ground.'

The fact that Angus had left his business at the early age of fifty-four did not mean that he was not fully involved in other activities. Until his death at the age of eighty-seven he daily attended an office where he employed two full-time secretaries and a part-time accountant. Although he refused a sequence of invitations to stand as a Liberal candidate for Parliament, he was prepared to be fully engaged in local politics. For many years he sat on the City Council and on two occasions served as Deputy Lord Mayor – he always refused the higher office. He was a leading participant in a number of charitable activities on Tyneside. He was a leading Justice of the Peace, and he took a close interest in the numerous companies in which he had a financial investment. Of these, the two in which he was most directly involved were the *Spectator*, in which he was the majority shareholder, and Ivor Nicholson and Watson, a firm of publishers which he founded ostensibly for the benefit of his sons who now were no longer able to take up their designated appointments as his successors in Angus Watson and Co.

But the *Spectator* and Nicholson and Watson require chapters to themselves.

CHAPTER TWO

NINETEEN THIRTY-FOUR, the year in which I put childish things behind me, was not a vintage one in which to launch out on a new career. The slump of 1931 had left its scars on industry. Unemployment was high. The Nazis were established in power in Germany. Already the probability of a forthcoming war was beginning to colour everyone's plans for the future. Those of my generation who were politically minded were shortly enlisting to fight in Spain which was to be the curtain-raiser to the main drama; those, the majority, who believed that war was over the horizon, continued to try to enjoy the few years that remained to them. I feel some shame that this was the course I followed. But the thirties, a decade of political betrayal and retreat, was too close to 1914–1918 for anyone of serving age to feel other than that his life was likely to be a short one.

I joined the firm of Ivor Nicholson and Watson in July of 1934 after finishing three agreeable years at Cambridge. It would be untrue to pretend that I had a burning ambition to be a publisher. When Angus's interest in his own business came to an end, and with it an assured succession for his sons, I had made the law my first choice of a profession. I allowed myself to be talked out of it. I remember a conversation with one of the leading barristers on the northern circuit with whom Angus had arranged a meeting. 'My boy,' he said, 'as a barrister you'll be lucky to earn as much as a bricklayer.' I did not stop to consider the fact that the conversation took place in a large house in a prosperous suburb of Newcastle. Angus then became active on the old-boy network and arranged for me a number of interviews with various business associates. But with the founding of Nicholson and Watson in 1931 I became increasingly enamoured of the glamorous life apparently being led by my elder brother Bernard in London. In those days Bernard had the sort of good looks and panâche that I much admired. His conversations about the book world became increasingly irresistible. I had always been brought up to believe that I would be working alongside Bernard in a family business and Nicholson and Watson, in this respect, was not all that different from Angus Watson and Company Limited. The disadvantages of such a paternal and fraternal arrangement did not become apparent until quite a lot later. Publishing appeared to present a more attractive image than the likely alternatives. So without much thought I became a member of the book trade.

The firm of Nicholson and Watson or, as it was originally called, Ivor Nicholson and Watson, originally consisted of Ivor Nicholson and my brother Bernard, finance being provided by Angus. The original capital was thirty thousand pounds, a more than adequate financial base for a new publisher. Primarily, the firm had been founded to give employment to Bernard who had been deprived of a job when Angus resigned from his business. Angus, for some reason, always felt a measure of guilt for this imagined deprivation for his sons. Bernard's partner, Nicholson, was a Welshman of exceptional good looks and charm. He had spent his professional life managing the magazines owned by Cassell, after which he became the London representative of Hearst Publications, the huge American publishing group which owned *Good Housekeeping* and other female-oriented magazines. Much of Ivor's time and energies were exhausted in fulfilling the more bizarre ambitions of the tycoon Hearst who thought nothing of purchasing on a whim, an entire Spanish castle and having it shipped, stone by stone, to California, where it remained unassembled in San Simeon where he resided with his mistress, the film star Marion Davies. Ivor once stayed in one of the guest houses at San Simeon. He used to recall with horror the Wurlitzer organ music which was piped through every room, precursor of today's Muzak.

Angus, who was one of the most successful businessmen of his generation, and who was the architect of a considerable commercial empire, demonstrated on several important occasions throughout his life an exceptional gift for making dotty decisions. As I shall suggest in a later chapter, he made one in his sale of the *Spectator*. There is not much doubt that he made another in approving the initial arrangements for his new publishing company. One requirement of an obvious nature was to balance the inexperience of Bernard by employing a man of proven book-publishing ability. The magazine-oriented Ivor was almost an equal innocent in the world of books. If it was not altogether a case of the blind leading the blind, at least it was a case of the blind man being given a guide dog with only one eye.

However, both Ivor and Bernard were determined to cut a swathe with the ample resources available to them. The Savoy Grill became their regular eating house. Every literary agent in London beat a path to the door of 44 Essex Street where cheques against advances for authors of no especial proven sales ability were being handed out to all comers. A new dawn of plenty appeared to have broken on the London book scene. Nor were authors the only benefactors. Victor Gollancz had pioneered the practice of buying huge areas of advertising in the book pages of the Sunday papers. What Gollancz could do well, Nicholson and Watson could do better. Huge promotional campaigns were mounted in the pages of *The Sunday Times* and *Observer*. The book trade sat up. Who, asked the gossips in the Garrick, were these spendthrifts?

As a matter of fact this money was not, by any means, all squandered. Ivor realized that generally the professional author with a regular output was under contract elsewhere. What was available to a newcomer, depending on the size of the cheque he could offer, was the one-book writer probably involved in writing his autobiography or some similar isolated venture. By paying over the commercial odds, Nicholson and Watson became the publishers of the memoirs of Lloyd George, Philip Snowden, Lord Esher, Ronald Storrs and many other famous persons. These books did much to establish the reputation of the new firm. For the six volumes of autobiography by David Lloyd George the firm made a guarantee of fifteen thousand pounds – in those days a huge outlay and, in fact, half their capital. But, contrary to general belief, it was the most profitable book the firm ever published and certainly did much to establish the imprint of this new and lusty company. In due course the list began to take on a more enduring aspect. Soon the foundations were laid for a series entitled The International Library of Christian Knowledge, published jointly with the American firm of Scribner's. It was administering this improbable undertaking – improbable, that is, that I should be in charge of it – that first brought me in touch with John Carter, the great bibliophile who, at the time, was Scribner's London representative, long before he crowned a distinguished career as the antiquarian expert at Sothebys.

Soon the first books were commissioned in a series which was designed to meet the growing needs of the Workers' Education Association. The editor was W. E. Williams, later to make his reputation as the inspiration behind the great Pelican non-fiction list.

But the shining jewel in the Nicholson and Watson crown was Stirling's projected *Bible for Today*. It is probably not an exaggeration to say that Angus might have had second thoughts about financing the new firm if his imagination had not been fired by this new bible which, from the very beginning, featured as its most important undertaking. John Stirling, its progenitor, was an ordained Methodist minister. He had a cosy personality and a sweet smile, not always to be found in practitioners of God. Through Angus's church connections, early rumours of Stirling's new project became known to him. Like many other schemes, all that was required was finance and Angus was eager to provide it. The intention was to produce a version of the Bible, making it a living document for the needs of the day. The authorized version would be untouched but explanatory and textual notes pointing up the modern relevance of each key passage would be printed in parallel columns beside the original. The pages would also be interleaved with numerous specially drawn illustrations, updating familiar Bible scenes and images. It was a major venture and an expensive one. It certainly captured the interest of Angus who regarded it as the most important item in the firm's plans. Increasingly it came to be regarded as the financial salvation of the company. But Stirling was not to be hurried. 'These things,' he pointed out, sucking his pipe and smiling sweetly, 'can't be rushed.' Indeed, they were not rushed. *The Bible for Today* was never to be published by Nicholson and Watson. When the firm was sold in 1940 the rights were bought by Oxford University Press. I believe their first edition was sixty thousand copies and they are reputed to have made a small fortune out of it. Salvation for the firm of Nicholson and Watson was not to come in this guise.

John Stirling, whom I loved, always reminded me of that story of the two tortoises who were dining in a pub; mother tortoise could not read the menu because she had left her glasses at home. Father tortoise said he would go and fetch them when he had finished his beer. After three days the lady began to complain of hunger. 'If you're in such a rush,' said father tortoise, 'you can go and fetch your glasses yourself.'

Another senior member of the firm was Burnard Phillips, a tall, angular man with a thin thatch of ginger hair and a wall eye. I believe he had been partially blinded in the First World War. He was a Cockney born and bred and, before he went into publishing, had been a horse-coper. He used to wear loud check suits and whistled through his teeth as if he was constantly grooming a horse. He was our sales manager.

Burnard, like many others of a fairly aggressive nature, found authority in any form offensive. He regarded it as a duty to deflate anyone in a uniform and the police in particular were his enemies. On one occasion I was with him watching a procession on its way to the Mansion House. We were standing on Ludgate Hill near our office. It was shortly after the army, for some reason best known to themselves, had decided to march in threes instead of the customary fours. When the marching escort arrived on

Ludgate Hill no one in authority had apparently noticed that the lamp standards were sited in the middle of the road instead of on the pavements. The soldiers, who would previously have divided round them two and two, virtually broke ranks. Some files split one to the left and two to the right of the lamp standards. Others broke in a reverse order. This caused some merriment amongst the onlookers and some consternation amongst the mounted police who were there to restrain the crowd. One policeman, safely seated on a huge horse, was suddenly seen gently to rear in the air. Perhaps the horse shared the general amusement. The disturbance – and it hardly rated the word – was momentary. But Phillips was out of the crowd like a flash. He grasped the bridle of the horse and shouted up at its police rider, 'You'd better get off that horse. I've a good mind to report you for riding to the danger of the public.'

On another occasion I was on a packed tube train at St Paul's station during the rush hour. Something or other – it wasn't difficult – got into Burnard. He reached up and pulled the communication cord. There was general consternation and, in due course, a station official arrived to explore the cause of the trouble. 'I demand that this carriage be partially cleared,' said Phillips. 'It is so full that it constitutes a danger to the public.' There was a good deal of fairly hostile muttering from the travelling workers who wanted to get home to a drink. Burnard fixed me with his basilisk stare and raised his voice. 'I'm sure you agree, Graham.' Aged twenty-three, I wanted to disappear into the ground.

The only other occasion when I have suffered from similar embarrassment on the Underground was much later. The train was equally crowded and, by chance, I found myself near but divided by a few bodies, from Lord Longford. Frank was an easily recognizable figure to the general public since he had recently received a great deal of publicity from his excursions into pornography. With some embarrassment on my part, but none on Frank's, we discussed a contract I was arranging on his behalf where he evidently considered the proposed royalties to be inadequate. The book was called, I recollect, *Humility*. Dear Frank, I also grew to love him and must relate one further recollection which really belongs to a later chapter.

We were dining at one of George Weidenfeld's huge dinner parties in honour, I think, of Elizabeth Longford. Before dinner I found myself in a huddle with Frank and Field Marshal Sir Gerald Templar who started to tell us an anecdote about his command in Newmarket in the early days of the war. 'And do you know,' he said, 'this fellow was behaving scandalously with the wives of fellow officers who were on duty overseas. So I called him in and I gave him a good dressing-down. "I'd shoot myself rather than behave like that," I told him. He left the room and three minutes later I heard a shot. The fellow was dead in the passage. Quite a good end, I thought.'

I still recall the mounting look of horror on Frank's face at the telling of this story.

The fourth executive member of Nicholson and Watson was Alan McGaw who joined us after resigning from the navy where he had served as a regular officer. His mother was a Tate, of Tate and Lyle, and his father had extensive interests in sheep-farming in Australia. Alan decided that the investment of some of his patronymy in publishing would be an entertaining, if not necessarily a profitable, way to use his money. Alan had a gift for design and he produced our books. He became a close friend and we shared a taste for girlie musicals featuring such male stars as Eddie Cantor which we watched in the Tivoli cinema, now replaced in the Strand by a branch of Peter Robinson. On certain nights we could be found supporting the lavish cabaret shows with which London in those days was well provided.

A further member of the staff who must be mentioned was my secretary-cum-assistant, Eleanor Hall. Eleanor and I provided the editorial functions of the firm. It is true that until his death in 1937, Ivor, in conjunction with Bernard, acquired the bulk of our important properties and they were the principal liaison with the agents but the day to day work of sorting out and dealing with the manuscripts, either bought or unsolicited, was Eleanor's and mine. We copy-edited them ready for the printer, we wrote the blurbs, we produced the catalogues and we dealt with any stray submissions.

But before I go into the slightly bizarre daily happenings at 44 Essex Street and then at 7 Paternoster Row behind St Paul's, I must digress to write about my time at Hazell, Watson and Viney, the printers, and Simpkin Marshall, the wholesale booksellers.

Before I officially joined the firm, Ivor, supported by Bernard, made a proposal to Angus that I should undergo a short apprenticeship elsewhere in the book trade. Whether this suggestion arose from the fact that neither of them had suffered such an apprenticeship, I do not know, but it was obviously a sensible idea and it appealed greatly to Angus who had been brought up in the Victorian tradition that a boy should endure at least a degree of hardship before he became a man. I hasten to add that there was little endurance involved in my six months at Hazell Watson and Viney, to be followed by three months at Simpkin Marshall. I would recommend a similar initiation for anyone entering the book trade and fortunate enough to have it offered to them.

Hazell's were top-grade book printers, situated in Aylesbury and then a family business. There were not, so far as I encountered them, any Watsons around and, indeed, I became most closely involved with Ralph Hazell and his family who lived in a handsome house in what was then still a small and attractive market town. Mr Hazell had two sons in the business, Raymond, a good deal older than me, and Peter, a contemporary who was naturally undertaking a much more intensive apprenticeship than was to be my lot. Peter and I quickly became close friends. His primary interest was in theatricals in which he had excelled at Cambridge, where he had also collected a blue for hockey. I remember the revue at the Footlights where the Cambridge University Rugby Fifteen came on to the stage dressed in lace pantaloons and kicking up their legs in unison as they sang, 'We are dainty little fairies, On our arms and legs no hair is.'

Peter looked very like the great Bobby Howes, one of the greatest of all musical comedy stars on whose personality he modelled himself. Later there was a moment when he had to choose between a professional career as an actor and being deprived of his family inheritance. Although I imagine this weapon was no more than a temporary threat, I think to his continuing regret he decided against the stage but, as a consolation, he threw himself wholeheartedly behind the firm's dramatic club which performed with near professional competence in a very handsome theatre built specially for the workers. Sadly, Peter was killed in the war.

Anyone with greater sense than I would have acquired a room in Aylesbury and lived there during the week. I was reluctant to leave the fleshpots of London and decided to travel down daily. This involved me in a schedule which entirely deprived me of the fleshpots which I was far too tired to enjoy. The works opened at seven-thirty a.m. By rising at five forty-five I was able to catch a train from Euston to Tring where I had left my car overnight. Motoring from Tring to Aylesbury I was able to get to the works by eight o'clock, for which I got no credit as my lateness was widely attributed to lying in after a rough night in London. In practice I arrived home exhausted and was in bed by ten o'clock.

Hazell's arranged for me to participate as an observer in every printing and binding process. I loved the craftsmanship that goes with producing a book and I found it fascinating to chat to the highly skilled workers who minded the machines. They had every reason to treat me as an extraneous nuisance but found some pleasure, I believe, in explaining their jobs to an interested by-stander. I greatly enjoyed my time at Aylesbury and have always been glad to possess even a very superficial knowledge of how a book is printed.

Simpkin Marshall was a wholesale bookseller situated in some labyrinthine buildings in Ave Maria Lane, in the City. They claimed to keep in stock copies of every book in print. Booksellers naturally used the service extensively. In London a customer could always be certain of obtaining his purchase within twenty-four hours of ordering and out of town booksellers within two or three days – in those years the parcel service was cheap and fast.

This stock of books was contained on miles of shelving, all carefully categorized. Each order, which was presented at the buying counter, was checked and then passed on to a 'looker-out' who disappeared into the murky interior from whence he reappeared in due course with the customer's books. Quite often these expeditions might last for some considerable time as one wandered with a basket past miles of shelving looking for some esoteric item. It was my theory that some lookers-out disappeared into the hinterland never to return, having died of fatigue or starvation after miles of walking . . .

It was an immensely slow, and not very efficient, system which could only be maintained because the wretched lookers-out were paid a beggarly wage. During the war Simpkin Marshall was bombed and although attempts were made to revive it they all foundered. Part of the reason for the appalling service now offered to the customer in the book trade is due to the absence of such wholesale booksellers, and I have never found anyone who could fully explain why, in Germany, for example, they are financially viable, but not, apparently, in dear, benighted England.

After a week or two with the lookers-out, accompanying them round the shelves on their leisurely excursions, I was transferred to the showroom which was a bookshop for use by booksellers and librarians wanting to examine current publications. At that time the twopenny library was flourishing and many of the owners found it convenient to order through Simpkin Marshall. Twopenny libraries were small ventures, usually to be found in sweetshops and tobacconists where there was a small stock of, mainly, popular fiction which was loaned out to customers. They were in competition with the big subscription libraries like Boots and W. H. Smith's which demanded some form of continuing membership. Both sorts virtually disappeared with the forthcoming mass-market paperbacks and the growth in usage of the rates-subsidized public libraries.

The showroom was run by Mr Nye who had as his assistant a friendly character called René Raymond. Shortly after my arrival both went down with flu and I was asked if I could cope alone.

Naturally I leapt at the opportunity and the first thing I did was to rationalize the exhibition of stock. I had noticed that most of our customers from the twopenny libraries were only interested in romance, sex and thrillers. These were dispersed alphabetically round the shelves. I organized them so that they were all together in one set of shelves. The saving in time was enormous. 'You'll find all the dirt on shelves 13–15,' I would say to the customer and he would beam his thanks at being saved so much time in making his selection.

I pointed out this popular innovation to Mr Nye and René when they returned. 'You know,' I said to René, 'one day some-one is going to make a fortune combining sex *and* violence.' Some months later René sent me an inscribed copy of his first book, *No Orchids for Miss Blandish,* under his pen name of James Hadley Chase.

But now I must return to Nicholson and Watson.

CHAPTER THREE

B Y 1935, the year in which I formally joined Nicholson and Watson after my apprenticeship, a good deal of steady list-building was in progress. Non-fiction is always easier to acquire than fiction and on this front quite a lot had been done in the hope of creating a continuing back-list on which the fortunes of any publishing house depend. Some of it was far from successful. W. E. Williams's programme for the adult student was going ahead under the title the University Extension Series. It included a number of admirable books but never really took off. Disappointing, also, were the sales of the International Library of Christian Knowledge, although Scribner's participation saved it from complete disaster. John Stirling, whilst progressing – if that is the word – with his work on *The Bible for Today*, produced other books under his aegis of which *The Story Atlas* was the least unsuccessful. Another future disaster centred on the formation of the Liberal Book Club in emulation of Victor Gollancz's Left Book Club. In spite of some distinguished contributors, such as Joyce Cary and Tom Harrisson, the tide was not running with Liberalism and the series lacked the passion of its highly successful counterpart.

But everything was not so gloomy. A series of guide-books devoted to each country in Europe and giving information on how the reader could spend a fortnight for the outlay of only ten pounds was a considerable success. A specially commissioned volume of essays by several distinguished contributors entitled *Great Victorians* hit the public's fancy and was followed by several others in a similar vein.

But success in non-fiction was essentially vested in the general books. Following in the wake of the big, expensive and successful memoirs of Lloyd George, Philip Snowden and Lord Esher were others which did well. Laura Knight wrote a first-class auto-biography called *Oil Paint and Grease Paint*. Clare Sheridan, cousin of Winston Churchill, had a success with the story of her life in the desert, *Arab Interlude*; E. Arnot Robertson, a well-known novelist, did a charming picture book called *Thames Portrait* and Pamela Frankau had a substantial success with her autobiography *I Find Four People* for which I had the pleasure of finding the title. *I Find Four People* was published at the moment when both the *Evening Standard* and the *Daily Mail* had started to promote their own Book of the Month. We were fortunate in gaining both selections in the same month – the first publisher to do so – with Pamela's book and Stephen Lawford's *Youth Uncharted*, an enchanting story of the author's Pimpernel experiences in the Balkans smuggling refugees out of the area. We made much of the joint occasion and the promotion included, for some bizarre reason, a reception on the much vaunted *Silver Jubilee*, a train which had just started running between London and Newcastle in the then record time of four hours. This occasion was good for publicity and also gave Bernard an opportunity for indulging his passion for trains, which was crowned for him by a specially arranged trip on the footplate of the engine.

Charles Graves, brother of the poet, Robert, and *Daily Mail* columnist, also joined the list about this time. Charles specialized in reporting the social world and I believe the resulting per-quisites far exceeded his royalties in value. On one occasion he was writing a book for us describing a journey through Europe, the expenses of which were being paid for by the manufacturer of the car in which he was travelling. Not unexpectedly the car had to be mentioned with some frequency in the text. Charles arranged to spend one night at the monastery on the Great St Bernard Pass, a privilege usually reserved only for travellers in distress. He dined in the refectory with the monks and was given a large bowl of pinkish soup. Out of politeness he commented on its quality.

'You must have some more,' said the prior, ladling in a further great spoonful. 'What is it made of?' enquired Charles. 'It's heated-up sheep's blood,' said the prior. Charles did not enjoy the rest of his meal.

But perhaps our most consistently successful non-fiction author was Rom Landau, a Pole who had settled in Great Britain. Rom was a great charmer and became the author of a number of books of which *God is My Adventure* is probably the best-known. This was an examination of a number of religious cults presided over by such men as Ouspensky, Gurdjieff and Krishnamurti. Rom was a great charmer and became the author of a number of Downs where he led a life nicely balanced between austerity and indulgence. He took his food seriously and, as a vegetarian, grew all his own vegetables. He meticulously followed a complicated programme of cultivation which included planting seed only when the moon was waxing. Whatever the rules they certainly worked. I often ate his garden peas in November.

After the war Rom got a professorship in some university in California. I am sure he would have had no difficulty in getting on with the hippies who, in the sixties, proliferated on the campus.

But, to get back to the firm, an important requirement, of course, was to build up the list of novelists, and to this we devoted much time and rather too much money. Amongst authors who joined us were Denise Robins, a hugely successful writer of romances, Philip Lindsay, Roland Pertwee, A. S. M. Hutchinson, Laurence Meynell and others then well-known but now mainly forgotten. I became immensely fond of Laurence Meynell, still a successful writer, and often stayed with him and his wife, Shirley, and a very asthmatic bull-dog named Watson, in my honour, whose nightly snores shook the rafters. Laurie lived a life of relative simplicity, but liberal hospitality. The guests were expected to work in the garden, chop wood and participate in long walks. The Meynells lived in a village above High Wycombe about twenty miles from London. One day Cyril Ritchard, an elegant, and successful musical comedy actor, came to lunch, with his wife Madge Elliott. Laurie and I came in from our work in the garden, took off our rubber boots and we all settled down for a drink in the comfortable but not luxurious sitting room. Cyril looked around at everything with great curiosity. He obviously felt he was a long way from the West End. 'Tell me, Laurie, what time does it get dark up here?' he enquired.

An author whom we did not publish was Frank Buchman, head of the Oxford Group, then a popular movement. At the time, the Group had an arrangement with the now defunct Metropole Hotel in Northumberland Avenue, just off Trafalgar Square, whereby Groupers could stay in the hotel for preferential rates. Some sceptics used to suggest that the hotel, as a quid pro quo, also used to make a substantial contribution to the movement's funds. One year Ivor decided that Dr Buchman ought to be persuaded to write his autobiography, so accordingly the two of us reported by appointment to his suite in the Metropole. 'Now,' said Ivor, when the preliminary discussions had been concluded, 'how much do you want by way of an advance?'

'I think,' said Dr Buchman, 'you should go away and pray to God and ask Him what He thinks you should offer.'

We went away and did our sums without the assistance of the Almighty, and came up with a figure of, I recall, £5000.

Next day we presented ourselves again at the Metropole.

'And did you do as I suggested?' asked Dr Buchman.

Ivor did not blink an eyelid. 'God told us to offer £5000,' he said.

Dr Buchman paused for a minute. 'I'm afraid,' he said gently, 'He told me to ask much more than that.'

Although Ivor, and to a degree Bernard, were the front men who flourished an open cheque book at the agents, there was plenty of editorial activity on the top floor where Eleanor Hall and I presided over the manuscripts. Stray offerings had to be glanced at before being rejected out of hand, a fate suffered by the vast majority, or dispatched to an outside reader for a critical report. Although about ninety-eight per cent of these unsolicited manuscripts were worthless – when I later became an agent I found this factor remained roughly constant – occasional nuggets were discovered amongst the sludge. I shall write in a later chapter about *Crippled Splendour* whose vast bulk was borne timorously up our narrow stairs by its nervous author. But there was Mary Fitt's *Three Sisters Flew Home*, the first novel by a writer who was to acquire a public and some acclaim with this, her first book. I wrote the blurb for *Three Sisters*, having already chosen the title, and was rewarded by a review in the *Observer* which virtually ignored the contents of the book but castigated the writer of the blurb for insensitive vulgarity. 'It is a terrible example,' thundered the reviewer, 'of *rus in blurbe*.' I confess my morale soared. Here was public notice.

Mary Fitt was the pen name for a university don in Wales who insisted on preserving her anonymity even from her publishers. When asked for a publicity photograph she produced a silhouette of her head photographed with the camera pointed straight at the sun.

Another unsolicited contribution was *Rotten Borough* by the anonymous Julian Pine. The book was a very funny, very bawdy novel about corruption and sex amongst the councillors of a small provincial town. Although the author sensibly wished to preserve his anonymity, being resident in the town concerned, he thought it would create publicity for his novel if he rang up the local paper and announced that the book was in fact about Grantham. The local paper quickly obtained a copy of the book and was delighted to make this local scandal its lead item; idle for us to protest that it was a work of fiction. We were saved from huge damages, I think, because no one actually wanted to admit that he was the original of one of the outrageous characters.

There were other stray callers. I remember a session with the notorious Aleister Crowley who was widely thought to live on an exclusive diet of grilled babies. Certainly there was an indefinable aura of evil about him. Then there was Count Potocki whose waist-long hair, sandalled feet and greasy robe were a familiar sight on the pavements of London – prewar precursor of today's hippies. And there was Ludwig Koch.

I am ashamed to write about Ludwig Koch because there can be no possible doubt but that Eleanor and I came out of the encounter exceedingly badly. Dr Koch arrived in my office carrying a rather battered portable gramophone, and some records in a carrier bag. Speaking in atrocious English with a strong German accent, he announced that he had made some remarkable recordings of bird song. His proposition was that they should be marketed in conjunction with an instructional book. I was, I admit, unimpressed by this opening. I was even more unimpressed by what was to follow. In those days gramophones were simple instruments without the veracity of tone which is standard today. Dr Koch's records were as basic as his gramophone. They scraped, how they scraped, as the squeaking turntable revolved. From time to time, between scrapes, there would come a peep-peep or even a couple of peep-peeps. Dr Koch, his hand cupped round his ear, would say, 'There, the golden-crested warbler . . . Hark, the lesser spotted missel-thrush . . .' I looked at Eleanor. Eleanor looked at me and I am afraid we both exploded with laughter. But Dr Koch had the last laugh. His bird-song, probably in a better recording, became a feature on the BBC and he went on to make a fortune.

Another side of our activities was the publication of a series of westerns. We used to do about twelve of these a year and we bought them in bulk from an agent. As they had all been previously published in America and as both Eleanor and I found them unreadable, we felt we must devise some means of taking the boredom out of readying them for the printer. We hit on the device of changing their titles, but without, I'm afraid, referring to the contents. Thus, for instance, *Lone Star Ranger* might become *Sheriff and Cowboy*. Or *Cattle Rustlers* might become *Pack that Gun, Pete*. Occasionally we received letters from our mystified readers who would querulously point out that there was no Pete in the book, much less a Pete with a gun.

In 1937 the firm suffered a stunning blow with the death of Ivor Nicholson. Still in his early forties he died of a long wasting illness.

We thought about a replacement, but none of us welcomed the idea of an outsider coming in to take charge of a business in which we had struggled for so long. However, by this time the question of finance was a constant preoccupation of the partners. Not only had we run through Angus's original capital but also the substantial additional money brought in by Alan McGaw. The firm was very near the point of making a profit but, by now, the forthcoming war was plain for all to see. Angus, understandably, was reluctant to increase his holding though equally reluctant to see the firm sink. For a time salvation looked as if it was to be found in the person of the Honourable John Willoughby, younger son of the Earl of Ancaster.

John's particular gift was playing the piano and he was never happier than when he was in a night club and could take over for an hour or two from the regular pianist. His father, the Earl, was the Lord Great Chamberlain of England. John's Bohemian tastes – and we were proposing that he should make a substantial investment in Nicholson and Watson – did not greatly appeal to him. I remember his suggestion that John should be put up for membership of The Bachelors, as he did not belong to any club – or not a club in the Earl's meaning of the word.

'But what point is there in joining a club?' asked John.

'Well,' said Lord Ancaster, 'you can go there and play bridge.'

'But I don't play bridge,' said John.

'Well, you can read a copy of the *Tatler*,' said the Earl.

'But I don't like the *Tatler*,' said John.

'Well, dammit, boy, where do you go for a pee?'

Before it was finally decided that no money was forthcoming from his father, John asked me down for a weekend to the family home of Grimthorpe, a vast mansion near Grantham. I confess that I was totally over-awed by the occasion. I felt my clothes were inadequate (we seemed to change them every few hours), I neither played bridge, nor shot, the two activities indulged in by the rest of the house party, and I knew none of the other guests. Panic-stricken, I arranged for a telegram to be sent summoning me urgently back to London. Trains on Sunday were few and far between but the Earl of Ancaster turned out to have the right to stop any southbound express at Little Bytham, his local station. Accordingly it was arranged that the Leeds-King's Cross express be flagged to a halt so that I could join it. Passengers peered curiously out of the windows to see the cause of this unscheduled stop. The driver expressed audible displeasure at being delayed on the fastest piece of track on the London North Eastern Railway. I was appalled at what had been arranged on my behalf. I knew my suitcase did not measure up to the occasion. Nor did a third-class return ticket, burning a hole in my pocket. With what resolution I could muster I walked towards a first-class carriage. Some honour, at least, had been salvaged from the weekend.

But with the Earl of Ancaster sensibly deciding that the aristocracy would not rescue the media from its difficulties, we drifted rudderless towards Armageddon. Alan was on the Naval Reserve. I was twenty-five and determined that I should confront the forthcoming conflagration in some kind of uniform. Meanwhile, Angus kept us going with a further relatively small injection of capital. Profit, achieved for the first time in 1938, seemed to lighten a little the gathering gloom.

No one who lived through them is likely to forget the eighteen months leading up to the war. The apotheosis of despair was reached with Chamberlain's visit to Munich. At the time I was on jury service at Newington Causeway. Several would-be jurors obtained exemption on the grounds that they had received call-up papers for the Territorials. As one walked through the park one could see trenches being dug, receptacles, said the gossips, for the two million cardboard coffins which were reportedly being made available for the first round of casualties.

The night of Chamberlain's return I happened to be dining at the Royal Automobile Club with Harry Greenwall, notable foreign correspondent of the *Daily Express*. Harry had just returned from Paris where he had been interviewing Madame Tabouis, a respected observer of the political scene, famous for her Cassandra-like prognostications. Harry, as a result of his interview, was in a state of extreme depression and by midnight we had both decided, not unaided by a modicum of alcohol, that further in-action in the face of this crisis was intolerable. So we climbed into a taxi, drove along the Embankment and mounted the gangplank of HMS *Enterprise*, London headquarters of the RNVR. The ship, whilst brightly lit, was deserted. However, we made our presence known and, in due course, an irate petty officer appeared on deck in his pyjamas. We informed him that we had come to enlist in the navy. We were given our congé after a short exchange about the navy never sleeping although, as we pointed out, HMS *Enterprise* appeared to be an exception to the rule.

Next day, sobered up, I pursued the attempt to enlist but, as I was to discover over the following eighteen months, the Services were not falling over themselves to take on anyone with less than perfect eyesight.

By this time there was an autumnal feeling in the book world. It was hard to concentrate on the discovery of would-be best-sellers when one knew that if they were ever published, which seemed unlikely, it would be by other hands.

On Sunday, 3 September 1939, we were all in the office listen-ing to Mr Chamberlain declare war on Germany. As we walked home through the empty streets the siren sounded and that night I enlisted in the Women's Voluntary Services, reporting to Dolphin Square, Victoria, to drive an auxiliary ambulance. Such attempts as I had made to get into uniform had been rebuffed and when the war actually started I happened to notice that the WVS were advertising for drivers of either sex. It seemed better than sitting at home and doing nothing.

For fourteen days we sat in Dolphin Square, polishing the vans which had been commissioned as auxiliary ambulances and learn-ing the street names round Victoria. For fourteen days we waited for an air raid which never happened. The Phoney War had begun.

So I returned to Paternoster Row, but our course was set. Alan had already returned to the navy. I had managed to get accepted into the artillery through the lucky chance that the doctor at the recruitment centre was the father of a friend of mine at school. Without testing them he readily agreed to accept my assurance that there was nothing wrong with my eyes. Poor Bernard was left to dispose of our assets and the firm was sold to a printer who, like all other publishers, made a fortune during the war, when almost any book found a ready buyer. Shortly after the war, when competition returned to the book trade, Nicholson and Watson ceased to exist.

But by then my life had been cast in another mould.

CHAPTER FOUR

THERE is a tradition, well-observed according to my observation, whereby those who were in the services during the
war seldom talk about their experiences. As those years were, for
most, the nearest one was ever likely to come to genuine adventure, such reticence is perhaps a little odd. It arises, I think,
because those who were on active service feel that to talk about it
to those who were homebound would verge on immodesty. And
those who were homebound, however disagreeable the civilian
experience, feel at a disadvantage when confronted by those who
wore uniform overseas. I propose to break that tradition, laying
myself open to I know not what charges, not because my war was,
in any sense, either heroic or of much general interest, but because
in a book such as this it would be absurd to ignore a period of
some consequence for the author. After six years campaigning
almost continuously abroad I returned, as did so many others, to
a world in which my job had disappeared, in which my civilian
contacts had disintegrated, and to a trade, in which I had a minor
skill, changed beyond recognition. Within six months I was to
acquire a wife, a job, a house and a completely new environment.
But it took a little time to adjust to the post war rhythm.

My lucky acceptance into the artillery, which I have already
described, led me subsequently to Brighton in the late spring of
1940. The recruiting sergeant in Merton, where I had rather
improbably been directed to sign up for the King's Shilling,
assured me confidently that the 21st Artillery Survey Regiment,
to which I had been assigned, was filled with highly skilled men. I
foolishly made no attempt to discover to what skills he was alluding

and so arrived at Preston Barracks, Brighton, with my hair shorter than it had been since leaving school and in total ignorance of what lay ahead. After checking in at the guard-room I was directed to a small chamber dominated by a large blackboard and filled with school desks. I was given a piece of paper and requested to answer the half dozen questions written out on the blackboard. I could see they embraced aspects of trigonometry and geometry and I felt there was little point in floundering around trying to resolve something far beyond my capacity. My education at Repton had ceased at an early age and it had never at any point taken in trigonometry. Accordingly I handed in a blank sheet of paper. I had not joined the army to become a mathematician.

Next day, having had my hair further shaven to a military length and been kitted out in khaki, we new recruits, some two hundred strong, paraded before the commanding officer. Twenty names, mine included, were read out and their possessors were commanded to step out of the ranks.

'You men,' said the colonel, 'were not able to reach the required level in the preliminary examination and are accordingly posted to the cookhouse. The remainder will start their training in artillery survey.'

If the authorities had set out to discover a foolproof way of persuading recruits to undertake a crash course in trigonometry they had certainly found one. I quite enjoyed my month in the cookhouse but it seemed a poor way to pass the ensuing years in the army, so my days quickly took on a routine whereby, when our basic daily drilling was over and our boots boned and spat to the required degree of polish, I sat on my blankets trying to ingest the elementary rules of sine, cosine and tangent. If release from cleaning greasy pans depended on the acquisition of knowledge about angles, such knowledge I was determined to acquire as fast as possible. By the time of the next monthly intake I had persuaded the authorities that I was ready to sit the test again. It is probably the only examination which I have ever passed with a hundred per cent success. But then the questions were relatively simple once you knew how to answer them.

The recruiting sergeant was true to his word. The men of the 21st Artillery Survey Regiment did, indeed, possess a multitude of skills. The authorities rightly considered that the ability to drop a battery of guns into action, plot their position on the map to the accuracy of sixteen coordinates – or a matter of feet in spacial terms – and then work out the appropriate range and elevation to the designated target required at least a modicum of intelligence. In consequence the unit consisted of a motley selection of individuals, many university trained, who took reluctantly to the discipline that the regular army sergeants sought to impose on us raw recruits. The attitude was, perhaps, exemplified by Gunner Robinson.

Gunner Robinson had a large and rather protuberant belly. One day, early in our training, we were on parade for inspection by a visiting colonel. We had just been given gaiters to replace the original issue puttees and felt rather pleased with our appearance. The Colonel walked down the ranks according to custom and we all stared in front, as instructed, with glazed eyes. The colonel stopped in front of Robinson. He obviously regarded himself as something of a wit. He prodded the gunner in the stomach with his swagger stick and said, 'Beer, I suppose?' Gunner Robinson continued to look to the front. His eyes remained glassy.

The colonel, unwisely as it transpired, poked him again in the stomach. 'I said, beer, I suppose?' He didn't know how far he was pushing his luck.

'Yes, sir,' said Gunner Robinson. 'And there's a tap underneath if you want to draw some off.'

Quite soon we had our training interrupted by the need to defend the coast from invasion. Rifles were requisitioned from the OTC of the nearby school of Lancing, sandbags were filled from Brighton beach and a guard was nightly mounted on the front of the pier.

Our regimental sergeant-major, never a man to consider that his charges were distinguishable from a 'terrible load of old crap', as he often addressed us, felt that at least some attempt

43

might be made to emulate the drill performed in front of Buckingham Palace. So nightly we put on a tremendous performance for the benefit of the locals who, deprived of their usual pierrot shows, crowded round to watch and even applaud. One night the dramatic tension was diminished when a kindly old lady advanced and impaled an apple on the bayonet of the relieving sentry. I used to enjoy these occasions, as I did manning the posts where, at night, we stared out over the channel through the darkness. God knows what we would have done with the antiquated Lancing rifles if we had ever had the need to use them.

In due time the invasion scare was over, our training was complete, the regiment moved to Larkhill on Salisbury Plain and our enjoyable days at Brighton were behind us. We were now fully-fledged artillery surveyors and applications were soon going in for commissions. My papers, in due course, were sent forward to the appropriate authority, by which time we had moved on to Burton-on-Trent where we spent our time billeted on a brewery floor devoid of hops, but not of their smell. I bided my time patiently awaiting my posting to an Officer Cadet Training Unit, but these were the days before the computer controlled our lives and a posting, when it finally arrived, turned out to be for an unknown destination overseas. I took my embarkation leave in Newcastle, a sad few days reminding me forcibly of the periods immediately before my return to school, at the end of the holidays. It was hard to believe that the family would ever reassemble in the years ahead.

I was due to catch a train to London at ten-thirty in the evening. During the morning it started to snow. By seven o'clock the streets were too deep in snow for wheeled traffic. I plodded down the four miles to the Central Station, my legs encased in the brown paper my mother had insisted on as a protection against the snow. I could not help feeling that in the years to come I would need more than brown paper to protect me from the ills of the world.

As it happened, the train, also, had problems with the weather. The journey to London took twenty-three hours.

I had further time to kill in Woolwich Barracks. The authorities made virtually no attempt to impose discipline on those awaiting an overseas draft and in the evening the barracks emptied as everyone made for London. I remember those journeys by tram through the almost nightly air raids, holding my tin hat over the lower part of my anatomy. I had no wish to survive the war with a high treble voice.

Early in February, 1941, we entrained for Gouroch where a vast convoy of ships was assembled in the Loch. No one knew our destination though as we had been issued with tropical clothing, it was likely to be Egypt or India, the principal active theatres of war just then. I embarked, a member of a small reinforcement draft of gunners, on the French liner *Pasteur*, newly commissioned just before the outbreak of war. The ship contained a motley cross-section of the army. A battalion of the Black Watch went out as a single unit, there were large detachments of signals and engineers and the majority of us were designated as reinforcements for units already engaged in campaigning. There was only one other artillery surveyor in my draft and I had only a slight acquaintanceship with the other gunners.

I confess that I did not enjoy my six weeks on the *Pasteur*. Except for the public rooms and cabins on the promenade deck the interior of the ship had virtually been gutted. We were assigned a dark, hot mess deck not far from the engines where we were supposed to hang our hammocks, eat our food and spend the better part of the day and night. The conditions were appalling and made no better by the knowledge that the commissioned ranks and a large detachment of nurses were housed in the prewar state rooms. It is difficult to imagine how the authorities could have allowed such a disparity between the ranks to come about and I believe the distinctions were later modified. On the *Pasteur* there was not, as there might have been, an organized mutiny but all the other ranks, unbidden, quickly abandoned their allotted mess decks, removed their bedding to any part of the upper decks where they could find a space and remained there for the remainder of the voyage. I slept outside the lift shaft on 'A' deck. The authorities sensibly made no effort to restore a situation which they knew was already beyond their control.

Morale was not improved by the food, which was disgusting. As we sailed through the tropics the main meal we were served most often continued to be mutton, cabbage, potatoes and plum duff! To augment these unpalatable meals we had to queue for three hours each day before the NAAFI counter where one was rewarded for the wait with a bar of chocolate, an apple and a packet of biscuits. Reports, via the cooks, of the refrigerated food being consumed by the officers in the first-class saloon did nothing to restore our spirits.

Of course, there was nothing to do on board except lie on one's mattress reading, talking and playing cards. The huge convoy did a vast sweep out into the Atlantic to avoid the waiting submarine patrols and after ten days we arrived for refuelling at the West African port of Freetown. A swarm of natives put out from the shore to be showered with pennies for which they dived for our amusement, but we were not allowed to land. A week later we arrived in Cape Town. Here we were to spend five days while the ships replenished their stores.

I shall always remember Cape Town with affection. Those of Boer extraction were noticeable by their absence but the Anglo-Saxons descended on the convoy in their thousands to offer entertainment and hospitality. After five days in a city where the war seemed a distant fantasy, and prewar conditions still existed, we were soon on our way again. Our destination was now known to be Egypt and, before long, weakened by too little food and too little exercise, we were sailing through the Red Sea to Port Suez. A little later we gunners travelled to the camp of Almaza, in the desert on the outskirts of Cairo.

Here the war began to take on a more vivid shape. Between the tents strolled bronzed warriors in sweat-stained shirts and tight shorts, temporarily absent for various reasons from 'the blue', as the desert was universally known. One watched them with a speculative air and listened to their tales. We knew that quite soon we, too, would be 'up the blue'. And, indeed, within days I was given a posting to the Second Regiment of the Royal Horse Artillery, one of the crack regiments of the British Army.

Anyone who is interested can read a number of excellent books about the desert campaign and I only intend to follow it in purely personal terms. But it is well known that for some years our tanks and anti-tank guns were hopelessly inferior to those of the Germans and Italians. The 2nd RHA was an anti-tank unit armed with two-pounder anti-tank guns mounted on open lorries and virtually without any armoured protection. The range of their guns was so limited that their fire had to be withheld until the opposing tank was within quite short range. The life expectancy of those who manned these weapons was generally agreed to be poor. My posting was, therefore, received by my companions with some commiseration.

We reinforcements were due to catch a train to the desert terminus of Mersa Matruh at ten o'clock in the evening. By lunch time I lay in the tent feeling as if I had been heavily beaten all over. By mid-afternoon I knew I was running a high fever. My companions urged me to report sick but I could not bring myself to take any action which might be thought to have to do with avoiding an unpopular posting. I decided, literally and meta-phorically, to sweat it out. But my tent mates thought otherwise. One of them fetched a doctor. He found my temperature was 104° and diagnosed a bad attack of sand-fly fever. So I found my-self in Cairo General Hospital instead of on the train to Mersa Matruh.

Back in Almaza three weeks later I was posted to C Battery, the Fourth Regiment of the Royal Horse Artillery, a sister unit to the 2nd RHA, but one armed with twenty-five-pounder guns, one of the most useful all-purpose weapons of the war.

A small reinforcement batch of gunners, all of us newly arrived from England, reached the battery on one of the lorries that nightly took petrol, ammunition and rations to the forward troops. We were the first civilian reinforcement for the 4th RHA, a regular regiment that had, until recently, spent some years in India, where horses were still being used for pulling the guns. We were inspected critically by these seasoned veterans and, because we had arrived at night and were wearing solar topees, were instantly christened the 'moon men'. It took us only a few moments to abandon our ludicrous headgear which I never again saw worn anywhere except by the base staff in the Delta. Dress in the desert was most often just a pair of shorts.

In those days, the spring of 1941, the forward troops were organized in so-called Jock Columns, named after their inventor, the famous Colonel Jock Campbell, Commander of the 4th RHA. They were a highly mobile force consisting of a troop of twenty-five-pounder guns, with supporting infantry mounted in Bren carriers, a couple of anti-aircraft guns and a troop of anti-tank guns. Their task was to keep in touch with the opposition, harass them if necessary but not be involved in any serious hostility. They operated a hundred miles or so in front of the main army which was regrouping in the area of Mersa Matruh, a small, by now demolished, town on the Egyptian coast. Every night the Jock Columns withdrew some miles into laager, a South African word meaning a group of vehicles, where they met up with the supply lorries which had come up from the rear areas. Every morning at first light the columns moved forward again to some newly allotted position.

My first contact with the sharp end of war occurred shortly after my arrival when the British made one of their many abortive onslaughts in a short-lived and unsuccessful action named Operation Battleaxe. At the time I was assigned to an ammunition lorry and my first taste of hostilities was being dive-bombed. The driver, long experienced in the ways of the desert, dived underneath the lorry. I followed him quickly. It was only afterwards that I wondered whether it really made an ideal bomb shelter.

With Battleaxe behind us, calm once more descended on the desert. By now I had been appointed assistant to the troop commander, who carried out the function of Observation Post Officer. The observation post was an unarmoured, eight hundredweight truck manned by the OP officer, his assistant (the OP ack), a signaller, who maintained wireless contact with the guns, and the driver. We four lived together, ate together, slept together and worked together and we became a closely integrated little unit. Our task was to get into a position where we could observe enemy activity and, if necessary, direct the fire of the twenty-five-pounders positioned some ten miles behind us. For protection we had a Bren carrier containing a dozen members of the Rifle Brigade and one anti-tank gun mounted on its lorry or 'portée'. Of course, the Germans were perfectly well aware of the function being carried out by these three vehicles, isolated as they were in miles of empty desert. As a rule they left us in peace, as we did them, for this was a period in the desert war when both sides were building up for the campaign we knew to be coming. Occasion-ally, however, we received attention from a dive-bombing Stuka. At the sound of an approaching aeroplane we would leap from our vehicles and take refuge behind a foot-high piece of scrub thirty yards away. The belief that the scrub provided any protection was illusory but, although we were clearly visible to the pilot as we lay prostrate on the floor of the desert, they never bothered to open up with their machine guns.

In the afternoons the heat would create a shimmering mirage from which curious shapes would seem to emerge. It was sleeping time and only one of us would keep a desultory watch from the roof of the truck. Occasionally a German vehicle which had lost its bearing would emerge from the haze and sheer quickly away. Once a German soldier peered into the back of the truck, unaware that it was British. It didn't occur to anybody to pick him off as he quickly disappeared on his motor-cycle. It was, at that time, a rather peaceable war, more akin, perhaps, to a naval battle with ships idly probing each other's strength. The wide, flat empty expanse of the desert, devoid of all life except for the ubiquitous flies which made life a nightmare, exerted a strong fascination. Before going to sleep, as one lay on the ground beside the truck one stared up at the purple sky with its shooting stars and listened to the quiet droning of the voices in the laager. But the nights were short. The guns remained in position till last light and had to be back in position by dawn. By the time one had eaten the evening meal and performed the several daily duties there was seldom time for more than four or five hours' sleep.

And so the summer and early autumn passed in relative calm with one short break when C Battery had a few days rest by the sea near Sidi Barani. By November the two armies were once more ready to engage. The main objectives of the British were firstly to relieve the garrison of Tobruk and then to advance across Cyrenaica towards Tripoli. Operation Crusader, supported by a hugely reinforced army, was launched in November. My most vivid recollection of this campaign was of two days of the battle of Sidi Rezegh which, compared to battles fought later in the war, may have been on a relatively small scale but which seemed to lack nothing in bloody ferocity. Our little eight-hundredweight truck seemed to be right in the middle of a considerable tank battle which, when night fell, left the horizon encircled by burning tanks and vehicles. I best recall two episodes. One was of a 2nd RHA portée, its crew stripped to their waists, some dead, the rest bloodily dying, lying mangled round the useless gun. The other was of a young officer, to whom we gave a lift on our way to laager, standing weeping beside the burning tank in which his crew had been incinerated.

Christmas, after two months' fighting, found us in Benghazi. We celebrated with a bottle of beer and some soya-bean sausages, brought up in the rations to reinforce the otherwise perpetual diet of bully beef and biscuits. In January we were relieved and the regiment headed back to Cairo for leave, rest and refitting.

I remember still the taste of that first iced bottle of beer and the cool spouting water of the shower on one's matted hair and bronzed body. And I remember the little Egyptian hotel where I and my companion fetched up on leave. It was completely full, as was all Cairo, and we were offered a mattress each on tables in the dining room. We returned very late, and very much the worse for wear, and fell into a heavy sleep. I awoke to the sound of conversation. The room was full of Egyptians having breakfast.

I lay naked to the world, the sheet which had been covering me having fallen beside me on the floor.

Our stay in the delta was brief. The troops who had relieved us were new to the ways of the desert and were once more in retreat. They were driven all the way back to the fortified line at Gazala, not far from Tobruk. Here both sides paused for breath. Our new role was to man a fortified 'box' deep in the south below the Gazala line, near Bir Hacheim, which was soon to get notoriety in the world's press through its suicidal defence by the Free French. In May the Germans suddenly struck round this southern flank and what came to be known sardonically amongst the troops as the Gazala Gallop had begun. If the powers that be guessed at the enemy's intentions, it is fair to say that we didn't. I still remember the surprise of suddenly finding ourselves next to a German staff car with a soldier poking a gun at us and saying, 'You are my prisoners.' 'Oh, fuck off,' said the sergeant in charge of our truck. And fuck off they did, and so did we. I never knew why the Germans didn't fire at our disappearing backs.

The ensuing days of retreat to El Alamein are well chronicled. They were depressing for those who took part. So much ground had been won. And now so much ground had been lost. Morale was at a low ebb. In due course we all settled down on the strong defensive line which stretched from the coast at El Alamein to Qattara Depression, a bare forty miles from Alexandria. Here both forces paused for breath, the Germans and Italians with a supply line stretched to the limit, the British to reorganize and re-equip. C Battery once more occupied a position on the south of the line and from here got involved in the sharp and important battle of Alam el Halfa which took place in August. It was Rommel's last attempt to smash the British and my last engagement with the 4th RHA. Immediately thereafter I was informed that my papers, approving the application for a commission, made two years previously, had at last caught up with me. I was ordered to return forthwith to Alexandria.

At the time, and subsequently in retrospect, I was not convinced that changing the status of a lance-bombardier (acting and unpaid) for that of a second-lieutenant was a step in the right direction. I was proud to be a lowly member of such a distinguished and battle-proven regiment. My regret was compounded when I discovered that my accursed short sight meant that my medical category was down-graded. There was a certain irony in the thought that I had passed much of my war at an observation post where an essential requirement was reliable vision. Now I was down-graded medically so that only a commission in a less combative unit was open to me. So I was posted to an OCTU in Palestine to train in the ways of the Royal Army Service Corps.

Three months in the sybaritic surroundings of a camp near Haifa, where a prewar existence was still maintained, passed all too quickly. By December I was back up the desert reporting to the RASC of the 50th Division, newly arrived from England. Dress in the desert was casually unmartial and it was the fashion to wear big, untreated sheepskin coats stretching almost down to one's ankles. I bought one in Jerusalem to celebrate my commission and was wearing it when I reported to my new commanding officer. Fresh from England he was wearing a traditional khaki issue overcoat. 'Good God, woolly Watson,' he greeted me, and Woolly Watson I remained throughout the remainder of the war.

It would be tedious to follow my war in the desert to its conclusion in Tunis. Let me skip to an almond orchard outside Syracuse where I found myself after taking part in the invasion of Sicily in a small advance detachment well ahead of the main company, who were to follow later. These were idle days of swimming, and exploring the nearby villages by army truck. Our diet was eggs by the dozen, peaches, as many as we wanted, tomatoes and almonds, a far cry from previous desert rations. The sun shone, the war seemed bogged down in the plain of Catania and life was good. We used to bathe several times a day below our tiny camp set up in an almond orchard above the Mediterranean. One afternoon I decided to swim across the bay, a distance across its mouth of, perhaps, half a mile. When I was more than half way across, I was caught in a strong and unexpected current. I swam on and with difficulty reached the other side. I knew that I couldn't swim back.

I stopped to consider my position and did not much like it. Walking round the verge of the bay was impossible because of the rocks. I was naked, without a costume, and virtually blind without my glasses. I suppose it was a walk of about three miles that I eventually did, barefoot and naked, back to my orchard, and it involved passing through the main street of a Sicilian village. I was glad I could not see the expressions on the faces of the locals as they went about their daily business.

Sicily, in due course, was conquered and I was soon to find myself in the invasion of Italy across the narrow straits of Messina. For a time we stayed in Reggio Calabria where I organized and, God help me, participated in two quite successful concerts which we held in the main square of the town. I sang a rather subversive song which I had composed about the navigational inadequacies of my superior, known by all his command to be constantly getting lost in the desert. It was well received by the troops but probably did not quicken my promotion. But the attraction that unfailingly brought the locals to the beach was the daily act of two of our officers who would mount the roof of a pavilion built on a pier jutting out to sea. From here one did a beautiful swallow dive while the other, who always got the most applause, would jump straight in with one hand grasping his balls, the other grasping his nose. Such are the incidentals of war.

In November, 1943, we sailed for England to prepare for the invasion of Europe.

Of course it was marvellous to be home after nearly three years abroad. After the wining and the dining, preparations for D-Day went on apace. The great Field Marshal Montgomery himself came down to address us as we camped in a wood not far from Romsey. 'Battle-hardened warriors from the desert and Italy . . . Spear-head of the attack on fortress Europe . . . We'll knock the Hun for six out of his fortifications . . . ' Was there no one else in the bloody army capable of fighting except those who had been at it for three years?

June 5 was grey and windswept as we embarked on an American tank-landing craft. This was it then, the battle to which everything else had been but a prelude. I felt a strange sense of tranquillity. I could have done with a drink, but the American navy is dry. We made do with beakers of coffee.

We left Southampton Water on a grey evening and the cliffs of England, perhaps for the last time, disappeared in the gloom. Twelve hours later the coast of France was etched against the dawn light. To right, left and centre stretched a vast concourse of vessels. Arromanches, our goal, lay ahead, peaceful in the grey light. The battle was already being waged a little further inland. D-Day + 6, which meant six hours after the start of the invasion, when I was due to disembark, had seen the bridgehead gained. The invasion of Europe was on.

My initial task was to establish an ammunitions dump from which to supply the divisional artillery. There was not a great deal of choice of location in a still relatively restricted beach-head and I found an orchard a couple of miles outside the village of Arromanches where we remained until the general break-out began. Supplies, of one sort or another, first on a divisional, then on a corps level became my preoccupation for the remainder of my time in the army.

Orchards and the stench of dead cattle in Normandy, *bocage* round St Lô, stinking carnage in the Falaise gap, the triumphant dash through Belgium with the local populace lining the streets in delirium, some unpleasantness by the bridge at Nijmegen when we were bogged down in the advance on Arnhem – it's all in the books, or nearly all. A posting to 30 Corps, the crossing of the Rhine, the end of the war and life in Corps Headquarters at Nienburg in Germany . . . not much interest in telling.

And Dorothy – how does she come into this story? Well, I was as usual playing liar-dice and, as usual at that time of day, was fairly drunk on the local bootleg gin. Suddenly she appeared in the mess and I swear that all our hearts missed a beat at this picture of youthful loveliness. She was the driver of a visiting general and my colonel had persuaded him to let him dress her up in the red-tabs of a general officer. The ploy was for her to pretend to be a queen of the ATS come to arrange for a detachment of her ladies to be billeted in Nienburg. Dorothy was led into the general's mess for lunch and it's hard to believe that, even for a moment, were those hardened warriors deceived. And when the meal was over my colonel, may he be blessed, brought her over to our mess. We were married shortly after. We've been married ever since.

CHAPTER FIVE

Demobilized early in 1946, married immediately after, jobless and houseless, I joined the *Spectator* to the surprise of the staff and the astonishment of myself. It was a transition which demands some explanation.

In 1928 Angus had become the principal shareholder and proprietor of the *Spectator*. If this is thought to have been a slightly bizarre purchase, I doubt whether it was any more so than its subsequent ownership by Angus's successors, Ian Gilmour, lawyer, Harry Creighton, businessman, and Henry Keswick, exporter. In fact, in the last fifty years the common denominator of the proprietors of the *Spectator* has been an absence of any prior journalistic experience – possibly a factor in its plunge in circulation to its present level and the loss of such political and critical importance as it once possessed. As a matter of fact this situation was anticipated by one of the most influential of its earlier proprietors, St Loe Strachey, who set up a Trust specifically to control the ownership and policy of the paper. The Trust consisted of such distinguished personages as the Presidents of the Royal Historical and Law Societies together with the heads of four equally august bodies. All one can conclude is that either they took their duties lightly, or they did not have the power to enforce their decisions.

Angus's first contact with the *Spectator* dated back to the First World War. He was at that time – as he was to be throughout his life – deeply concerned at the national expenditure on alcohol and he became active with others in a movement to enforce wartime prohibition. As part of the publicity to bring this about, he approached St Loe Strachey, obtained his support, and a personal friendship developed. Although nothing came of the scheme to introduce wartime prohibition – and there were no plans to extend it beyond that limited period – a by-product of the campaign was the establishment of state ownership of the pubs in Carlisle where drunkenness amongst the munition workers was said to be running at a high level. This scheme, which had the support of the Temperance Movement, lingered on for years, but was never extended to other parts of the country.

Shortly before his death, St Loe Strachey wrote to Angus to discuss the future of the *Spectator*, of which he was then sole proprietor. It was believed he wished to keep the paper out of the hands of his son, John, then a communist. But for some reason the meeting never took place and when he died it was found that he had sold the bulk of his holding to Evelyn Wrench. The Strachey family, through John and his sister Amabel, who was married to the architect Clough Williams-Ellis, continued to own a small parcel of shares and were thus associated with Angus throughout the time when he was the main shareholder.

Evelyn Wrench, who was subsequently knighted, started his journalistic career as private secretary to the first Lord Northcliffe. He was an immensely good-looking, fastidious Irishman who, when I met him for the first time, lived in an elegant house in Chelsea. At that time I was at school at Repton and had journalistic ambitions. Angus arranged for me to have twenty-four hours' leave of absence to seek professional advice about making this my career and arranged that I should dine with Wrench and next day have an interview with Hamilton Fyfe, then editor of the *Daily Mail*. I do not remember what transpired at these conversations to turn me away from Fleet Street, but I do remember Evelyn Wrench, garbed in a plum-coloured velvet smoking-jacket, sitting beside his fire and stroking a large Persian cat. This image of the good life was to be refreshed when, as a publisher in later years, I was concerned with his two autobiographical volumes, *Uphill* and *Struggle*, which always rated high – and somewhat derisively – in the office as two of our most inappropriately titled books.

Wrench, though he came from a background where 'struggling uphill' was hardly a preoccupation, was nevertheless a dedicated man and, after some years as editor of the *Spectator*, he left journalism to found those successful organizations, the Overseas League and the English-Speaking Union. There was later to be a third, the All Peoples Association which ultimately foundered but which, at the time, was run by another endearing Irishman, Sir Christopher Robinson. I remember walking beside Kit through the arcades of the Ritz Hotel on the way to his premises in Arlington Street when his false teeth fell out. He caught them with the deftness of a gamesman, popped them back in his mouth without breaking his stride, or, so far as I could judge, pausing in his discourse.

It was, I think, Wrench's anxiety to press ahead with his plans in these other directions that caused him to respond favourably when Angus approached him about purchasing the whole, or part, of his share-holding. That such a thing should ever have entered Angus's head must surely rate as one of those silly schemes with which he tended to enliven an otherwise prosaic existence. Whenever he was asked what induced a man living three hundred miles away, without the slightest knowledge or experience of the newspaper world, to invest a considerable sum of money in a business which, financially, was barely making ends meet, he would reply that it was because his son, Bernard, soon to be out of a job because of the Lever takeover, had expressed a wish to go into journalism. I find this an unlikely explanation, partly because Bernard did not, in the event, join the *Spectator*, partly because at no time did he ever evince the slightest aptitude for journalism. What I think is the more probable reason is that Angus himself was interested in extending his contacts in the world of writers, a profession for which he had always had a Victorian respect, and he also foresaw the possibility of using the paper as a means of promoting those projects – temperance, liberalism, religion, social welfare – which were so dear to his heart. Whatever the reason he became the principal, if absentee, proprietor.

I emphasize the word absentee because there is no doubt that living in Newcastle made the exercise of any control difficult, especially as he was dealing, as a complete amateur, with a group of moderately experienced professionals. Of course, on Wrench's withdrawal from control, the first necessity was to find a new editor and the appointment was made of Wilson Harris who was then leader-writer and diplomatic correspondent of the *Daily News*, which later became the *News Chronicle* and subsequently passed into oblivion. He was to remain as editor into the early fifties and throughout this period the paper gained in circulation (especially during the war years) and, I think, in influence.

Students of literary magazines might compare the issues of the paper published in those terrible years leading up to the Second World War with those that were to be published thirty-five years later. Under Harris few articles were written by any but leading authorities, few letters were contributed except by correspondents instantly able to command a public platform. The reviews at the back of the paper were by well-known critics. Thirty-five years later the serious features have to compete for attention with advertisements which at one time were more likely to be found in newsagents' windows.

Harris, however, was not the easiest of men to work with nor, I suspect, an uncomplicated personality. I first got to know him moderately well in the thirties when, with my sister – I should say, perhaps, because of my sister – I was invited to naked swimming parties in the small pool in his country cottage near Dorking. He was a Quaker, gaunt, angular, intellectual, and if he possessed a sense of humour, which I doubt, he certainly lacked a sense of fun. Later, after the war, when I became a junior member of his staff I developed an antipathy for him which outlasted our actual relationship. It was only much later, looking back on his achievements, and comparing them with his successors', that I came to realize how hopelessly I had underrated his ability. He was incomparably the most able editor of the *Spectator* in the last half century. That is a judgement which may be challenged by supporters of Brian Inglis who had a brief reign under the proprietorship of Ian Gilmour in the fifties and, during it, gathered together at 99 Gower Street an assortment of previously unknown talent which included Bernard Levin, Katherine Whitehorn, Iain Hamilton, Alan Brien, Bamber Gascoigne and others who were later to make their mark in the national press. But there was a *gravitas* in Harris which was lacking throughout the Inglis régime.

Harris himself collected around him an extraordinarily impressive team of contributors. His literary editors in an unbroken stretch included Peter Fleming, Derek Verschoyle, Dilys Powell, Graham Greene and W. J. Turner. Harold Nicolson made his reputation as an essayist with a weekly piece which was later, on his retirement, to be taken over by Fleming, writing, at that time, under the pseudonym of Strix.

But it must reflect on the personality of Harris, as an employer, that most of these literary editors came to, and went from, 99 Gower Street with greater rapidity than would normally be accounted for by the demands of a career. Graham Greene once told me that he had tried to form an 'I hate Harris' dining club consisting of old Gower Street employees. Harris's policy of divide and rule paid few dividends in affection.

I remember rather clearly one day when, during my short period on the staff, I was passing the time of day with Walter Turner, literary editor and outspoken Australian poet. It should be explained that 99 Gower Street had, at some previous time in its career, served as a brothel. On to the garden, which conventionally extended from the rear of those late Georgian houses, had been built a two-storey addition divided into cubicles, each just able to contain a single bed and appropriate bedroom furniture. These cubicles were now used as offices for the secretaries and were so cramped that doors had to be kept permanently open – there wasn't the space to shut them in. On this occasion our conversation was interrupted by Harris who glided into Turner's office with some instruction about the coming issue.

Clearly he disapproved of what he saw and the rebuke was implicit. Turner waited until he was safely in the passage then, raising his voice a little so that the editor would miss not a syllable, he said, 'Graham, did you ever before see such a fucking shit?' You could feel the secretaries down the corridor turning up their collars at expletives which, in those relatively innocent days, were seldom heard.

But if Harris was disliked by his staff he was a formidable antagonist and adversary. He very quickly realized after his appointment as editor that it would be easy, and to his advantage, to drive a wedge between Wrench and Angus and keep a balance between the two men. Wrench, at this point – circumstances changed later – was content to leave Gower Street to its own devices. Angus, on the contrary, was anxious to play an active role in the direction of the paper but did not really know how to set about it. Inevitably, he was largely restricted to communication by post, and thus he did his best to react to the contents of the paper and provide suggestions as to its immediate future. Harris, however, had by this time taken the measure of the situation and, whilst he never actively encouraged a breach in the relationship, he never disguised his disinterest in the advice being proffered by this distant, journalistically inexperienced north-countryman. Although Angus continued to react to each issue throughout his proprietorship, the paper, with all its virtues and all its faults, was the sole creation of its editor. If this suggests that Harris rode roughshod over his proprietor it must also be admitted that Angus's letters were scarcely of a nature to stimulate an editor.

Looking back, I think that probably the only real fun Angus had from Gower Street was his involvement with the magazine *Everyman*, which flowered briefly in the attic of 99. *Everyman* was the brain-child of its editor, Francis Yeats-Brown, author of a best-selling book about his years in India called *Bengal Lancer*. Yeats-Brown became friendly with Angus and sometimes stayed with us in our house in Rothbury. I remember him standing on his head, seemingly for hours, in a corner of the sitting room, practising yoga. Yeats-Brown persuaded Angus to use the *Spectator* organization to publish a new magazine which Angus and others would finance. The intention was to produce something of light general interest which would capture a wide audience. One of the projected features was an 'Ask Uncle Wilfred' (or whatever the name was) column in which Uncle Wilfred would solve readers' problems. The idea has often been used in magazines and is nearly always popular. The burning question was who was to be Uncle Wilfred? Whether seriously or flippantly I do not know, Yeats-Brown persuaded Angus to take it on. I often planned to write a letter: 'Dear Uncle Wilfred, how do you race greyhounds?' to which I would get the answer, 'Dear Reader, you don't. You can't run fast enough.' Not a very good joke stolen from the repertoire of the great Billy Bennett, Almost a Gentleman. Oh, dear departed Music Hall!

Everyman survived a matter of weeks but there was a further bizarre episode before its demise. Complaints were received by the editor of the *Spectator* about a naked man seen through the windows of the top storey – and not only naked but standing on his head. Thus yoga came and went from Gower Street.

If Harris was the *Spectator* and if the *Spectator* spoke with a voice of authority which played a not unimportant part in the formation of public opinion, it was, by present-day practice, conducted from a very narrow base. Perhaps its most important running feature was 'A Spectator's Diary', contributed by Harris under the pen name of Janus. The diary might, perhaps, have been more enjoyable had it indeed been 'two-faced', but in fact it kept a pretty steady balance based on reasonably well-informed West End, Whitehall and City comment. The bulk of this gossip actually emanated from the Reform Club where, on most afternoons, Harris would be found after lunch in front of the fireplace in the upper smoking room surrounded by the same group of cronies, most of them academics, civil servants, journalists and politicians. In his wallet he kept a pasteboard postcard and on it was jotted in neat spidery handwriting the news, reflections and gossip which arose during these conversations and which ultimately became the basis of the week's paragraphs.

Most weeklies, nowadays, garner like trivia at crowded and, usually, drunken cocktail parties or lunches. But in Angus's day the policy inaugurated by St Loe Strachey of banning all liquor advertising and, of course, implementing where possible a similar ban in his personal and business relationships, made any such frivolling out of the question. But Harris's sources somehow added up to a solid feature and Janus was the most popular page in the paper.

Later, for a short time, I used to contribute some paragraphs to a column which provided comments on the week's news. In most instances my ignorance about the subject in hand was almost total, so on occasion I would ring up the press room of the government body concerned. For example, I would enquire of Guy Burgess at the Foreign Office, What was our line that week on China? This experience, and, later, personal acquaintance with a number of newspaper leader-writers, has left me with something of a credibility gap when the news is explained to the general public.

I suppose my later short journalistic career on the *Spectator* dated back to 1937. In that year Harris was running a series entitled The Voice of Under Thirty to which he invited me to contribute. I am sure at the time he had no notion I would later be on his staff. The series was anonymous and created sufficient interest for the articles and the resulting correspondence to be printed later as a booklet. I think I can claim that my article easily created the most baleful response. I had hoped to get under the skin of the largely middle-aged, middle-class readers by an attack on the inadequacies of conventional, established religion and how it was failing to appeal to the young of the day. Re-reading it, I must admit it was superficial, glib and self-satisfied but the hard core of the argument still bears up today.

Amongst its more unexpected results was that it was the beginning of a desultory connection with Harris which came to a head during the war. During the five years when I was on almost

continuous overseas service, I contributed an occasional article
to the paper in which I attempted to give some personal reflections on the life and thoughts of a soldier continuously away from
home. They appeared anonymously and their various attributions
– Captain MEF, Captain BLA, etc. – depended on the theatre of
war in which I was serving at the time. As a serviceman, one
was not allowed to write for the press. Some of the articles
appeared to attract attention and one in particular, which was
written from Germany in the latter days of the war, succeeded
in irritating a great many people and a booklet was produced
by the *Spectator* reprinting the article and correspondence arising
from it. However, it had for me a larger consequence, partly
because it was the reason, I think, for Harris agreeing that I
should join the paper on demobilization, partly because I
received a letter from Spedan Lewis commenting on it and
making a proposal about my future.

Spedan Lewis was the head of the chain of stores run by the
John Lewis Partnership and, before almost anyone else, had done
more than just talk about partnership in industry between
employers and employees, he had actually put theory into practice.
How it works in daily usage, and whether the staff either benefit
financially or have a genuine feeling of participation in the running of the business, are not matters on which I am competent to
judge. I do know that after my brief relationship with Lewis I
felt I had been in contact with a remarkable man.

After my article from Germany had appeared, I received a
four-page, typed, single-spaced letter from Lewis commenting on
the points I had made. With the general tenor and tone of my
arguments he appeared to be in agreement. He had read the other
articles from, he had guessed, a similar source. His organization,
with the return of peace, was in need of young men of questing
minds. If ever I should be interested, I was to get in touch with
him and he would offer me a job.

By this time I had committed my future to the *Spectator*. With
my demobilization pending and engaged to be married, Angus
was anxious that I should have a job when I left the army. Against

all the evidence (he had known me a long time) and presumably aware of my limited potentialities, he was, I know, entertaining a private ambition that I might one day become the editor of the paper or, at the very least, its managing director. For my part, I was prepared to acquiesce in his plans. I had not the slightest idea what I wanted to do or what I was capable of doing. During my five years of overseas service I had not given much thought to what was to come after the war. I had vaguely thought that I would probably stay in the same sort of world in which I had gained such limited experience as I possessed. Other than that I was ready to be persuaded. Angus persuaded me. And, having no better alternative to propose I became a member of the staff at 99 Gower Street. What my employment must have cost Harris in terms of having to agree to the employment of a quite unsuitable addition to his staff in order to accommodate a wish of his proprietor, I was only able to judge by his subsequent attitude. What it was going to cost me emotionally I was soon to learn.

The staff of the *Spectator* was small. Many of the contributors were part-time. Those who were full-time were a motley bunch who had few interests in common beyond dislike of the editor whose dictum for staff relations was divide and rule. After the companionship of the army I soon began to chafe at the isolation of Gower Street and it was not long before I remembered Spedan Lewis's invitation. I wrote to him and received a letter back which asked whether I would be interested in editing his house magazine, and what salary would I expect. At the time I was earning £650 a year but I saw no good reason why I should admit this. I replied that I was, indeed, very interested in his proposal and would require a salary of £2000 a year, which seemed to me more in accord with what I imagined was the going rate in Fleet Street. By return I received a letter inviting me to lunch at his house in Hampshire. So, with some little trepidation, I set off to meet what I hoped would be my future employer.

Spedan Lewis was waiting for me in the drive of his substantial country house, dressed, as I recall, in a Norfolk jacket and grey tweed knee-breeches. 'We'll take a walk,' he said.

For the next two hours we marched across the Hampshire fields whilst I was subjected to as searching a personal inquisition as I had ever experienced. 'It's the small things about a man which I notice,' said Lewis. 'I once got rid of one of my directors because he had dirty finger nails. It's things like that which reveal a man's character. The big defects can always be disguised for a time.' We returned to the house for a late lunch where the examination continued in front of three women who, I believe, were his secretaries and housekeeper and who contributed little to the discussion. 'Our house magazine,' said Lewis, 'is a vital link in my organization. Through its pages I keep in touch with my staff and the staff keep in touch with the management. It is the staff notice board on which anyone is entitled to pin an announcement. Through it I judge morale and through it I stimulate morale. As editor in a post so crucial to the Partnership, the salary you are asking, though substantially, I expect, greater than what you are earning with the *Spectator*, is perfectly reasonable.' I felt a small glow of satisfaction that my audacity was paying off and I started to wonder in what way Dorothy and I would change our life style. 'Now suppose,' continued Lewis, 'you were to receive an anonymous letter, would you print it?'

One of my duties at the *Spectator* was to deal with Letters to the Editor and we had a rigid rule that no unsigned correspondence would be published. What was good enough for the *Spectator* seemed to me good enough for the John Lewis Partnership and I replied accordingly. Shortly after lunch I returned to London.

A day or two later I received another closely typed and very long letter from Lewis. He had enjoyed our meeting, he wrote, and was only sorry that he was not going to offer me employment in his organization. But his decision had been reached when I had reacted to the key question of our discussion. 'Any editor with his finger on the pulse of public opinion in a closed society like the Partnership would instinctively have realized that it was anonymous letters which were the important ones as only thus could an opinion be freely expressed without its holder feeling that his job was thereby at risk. Someone so naïve about the ways of commercial life had better remain in the tranquil backwater of Gower Street.'

However, by this time my mind was made up to leave the tranquil backwater as soon as possible. Whatever the comparatively attractive prospects of a future secured by Angus's shareholding, the situation was too close a parallel to my employment at Nicholson and Watson where my position was also ultimately the result of parental investment. The time had come to prove to myself what my worth was on the open market. Early in 1947 I put an advertisement in the personal column of *The Times* and from it was offered employment by, amongst others, Curtis Brown, a firm of well-known literary agents which I was ultimately to serve for more than thirty years.

But I was not yet through with my bizarre association with 99 Gower Street. In 1951 Angus asked me whether I would return as a member of the Board to watch over his financial investment. By then it was fairly obvious that an editorial change could not long be postponed since Harris was in his late sixties and, although Angus and Wrench still took pains to maintain, on the surface, an amiable relationship, in fact their friendship was becoming increasingly strained.

After the successful establishment of the Overseas League and the English Speaking Union, Wrench was finding less and less to occupy his attention except routine management problems. During the war he had been absent from the country for long periods on various promotional tours; Angus, throughout the war, had been more than fully engaged as Divisional Food Officer for the north of England and Harris accordingly had been left a free hand to run the *Spectator* without proprietorial interference. The paper had prospered under his editorship and now he showed no signs of wanting to relinquish it. Wrench, however, was increasingly eager to get back into the editorial chair and solicited support from both the Stracheys and Angus. Angus, however, was not prepared to countenance any such change. Harris had kept things going during the difficult years when Wrench had been pursuing his own interests abroad and Angus regarded it as quite improper that he should now propose the compulsory retirement of Harris. Relationships between the two men deteriorated.

Although I did not sufficiently appreciate it at the time, I think my own relationship with Angus *vis-à-vis* the *Spectator* – and only in this connection – was also deteriorating. Until a very late date he had always entertained the hope that one day I would change my mind and return to Gower Street. Now all he garnered from his association with the paper was a continuing financial loss and a worry about the future. From time to time we had conversations about a possible course of action. I remember proposing Malcolm Muggeridge as editor before he joined *Punch* in that capacity. I remember arguing that there was no hope for the future unless the paper was turned into a Sunday publication like the *Observer*, keeping broadly to its existing features and getting the essential news from a service like the Press Association. But, understandably, Angus's heart was no longer in it and I also felt my own involvement gave me the worst of all worlds – responsibility without the power to protect it.

Nevertheless, I was quite unprepared for the shock of hearing, shortly after Harris had formally, and with much protest, retired from the editorship, that the paper had been sold. Without referring the matter to me, his nominal representative on the board, Angus met Wrench in the Station Hotel, York, and they jointly agreed to get rid of their holdings. Prior to this meeting Wrench had, with Angus's private agreement, approached Coutts, the bankers, about a potential buyer and Coutts had put them in touch with a young man called Ian Gilmour. Gilmour, later to become a pillar of the Tory party, was at that time a struggling, comparatively unknown barrister. Struggling is, perhaps, scarcely the *mot juste*, as his father was a wealthy businessman with close connections with Vaux, the brewers, and his wife was a daughter of the Duke of Buccleuch, one of the richest landowners in the country.

It seemed obvious to me that the only possible motive for

acquiring an ailing weekly such as the *Spectator* was to obtain for oneself a political or social platform. As the paper had always pursued a Liberal policy and as Angus was a life-long supporter of the Liberal party, I naturally questioned the wisdom of a sale to someone of probable Tory sympathies.

'There is no intention at all of Gilmour using the paper for political ambition,' said Angus. 'He assured me categorically he had no wish to enter politics.'

Gilmour, in fact, immediately took over the editorship from Walter Taplin who had been Harris's deputy and who, during this period, had been keeping the editorial chair occupied. Gilmour, in turn, after a year or two, hired Brian Inglis to succeed him as editor and Brian provided, I think, a sunset glow of at least provocative interest until, after his departure, the paper started its long slide.

As to myself and the Watson connection, I look back on years of wasted opportunity culminating in a manner of quitting which I still regret. I haven't much use for the amateur and there is no arguing that during Angus's proprietorship, only the professionalism of Harris gave it a voice to which those of power and consequence occasionally listened.

CHAPTER SIX

COVENT Garden, where Curtis Brown had their offices, was an immediate improvement on Gower Street. My job was running the American Book Department and this took me in 1948 on my first postwar trip to America. I travelled, in the company of Joan and Robert Lusty – at that time a partner in Michael Joseph – on the *Queen Elizabeth*. England was still enduring rationing and the deprivations of postwar existence percolated into every niche of one's life. The *Queen Elizabeth* was accordingly a revelation – particularly of one's capacity to eat! A vast breakfast at which passengers, or some passengers, tucked into porridge, kedgeree and kippers, followed perhaps by chops and steak, was followed at eleven o'clock with the offering of a cup of bouillon. Drinks at noon were an appetizer for the serious business of a huge luncheon after which one dropped into bloated sleep in preparation for tea, crumpets and cakes at four o'clock. But the serious moment of the day was drinks to be followed by a gargantuan dinner. And, before turning in, there was a plate of sandwiches in the smoking room for those who still felt peckish. Occasionally I still relive such voyages when confronted with the plastic trays offered by the air-lines when flying the Atlantic.

New York was a further revelation. My only previous visit had been in 1935 and I had forgotten that magical moment when the glow fades from the sky at dusk, the lights go on in the offices and the cavernous streets become canyons of mystery. Nor, of course, had America suffered any serious deprivations during the war and the feeling of profligate wealth and luxury was doubly stupefying after wartime England.

I stayed at the Chatham Hotel, now defunct, as are the Gladstone and the New Weston, my bases on future visits. Any hotel which has me on its books should look to its future prospects. Reference to the New Weston reminds me of the problem one sometimes encounters in New York in getting information about one's telephone messages and posts. On one particular occasion Mark Longman, who was staying at the New Weston, was sent, by our office, a parcel which was delivered by hand. In spite of a written receipt the hotel denied all knowledge of its acceptance and a thorough search was unavailing. Twelve months pass and Mark returns to New York. The hotel is the same, the sender is the same, the complaint is the same – but over another parcel. After a little time for search the hall porter advances, beaming. 'Ah, Mr Longman, here it is. We've found the parcel for you.' Mark opens it and finds inside, the manuscript which was missing from the previous year.

In the years immediately following the war, American publishing was still personal and independent – if not a cottage industry, as it was in Britain, at least no bigger than a respectable country craft. By and large firms were still controlled by proprietors who worked in them. The family business still existed. Small new firms could be founded and largely survived. The inexorable march to ownership by the anonymous accountant-controlled conglomerate had not yet begun. Publishing was still a matter of books and people rather than solely of profits. Furthermore, what was shortly to grow into a substantial transatlantic trade in the mutual exchange of rights was still in its infancy. Few American publishers found it worth their while to run their own overseas offices – that was to come later – but during and after the war, while the English were still adjusting to peace-time conditions, there was a ready market in Britain for books written by American authors. Curtis Brown thus became the representative of a wide range of American publishers and agents. In the late forties and early fifties they were selling annually to British publishers the rights in three hundred and fifty books of American origin.

As head of this American side of the business my job in New York, therefore, was to see the American publishers and agents we represented, find, if possible, new clients and meet our more important authors.

This agreeable assignment used to take five or six weeks each time, and this included two Atlantic crossings, a very different proposition from the two working weeks and two weekend flights of today. If the professional pace was nevertheless fairly hectic, the social pace was killing. Americans are famous for their hospitality and in those days they were not inundated by the constant stream of English who are currently a feature of the publishing scene. Then an Englishman was quite a rarity. Thus I had the good luck down the years to become very close friends, not only with a number of American publishers and agents, but also with some of the best-known American writers.

It was on this first trip that I met Anya Seton, for instance. Anya then lived, as she does now, in a charming house in Greenwich looking out over Long Island Sound. We immediately discovered a common bond in that her father, the well-known naturalist writer, Ernest Thompson Seton, came from Tyneside. A little after this encounter Anya was to embark on one of her better-known novels, *Katherine*, which required intensive research in England. It was still relatively soon after the end of the war but we in England regarded the country as having returned more or less to prewar normality. Anya, however, obviously felt she was visiting a still beleaguered citadel, and she wrote anxiously about the availability of Kleenex, lavatory paper, and other essentials for the good life. At the same time she asked whether I could provide her with a letter of introduction which would open the various doors where she needed to do research. I was not at all sure that any letter of mine would achieve such an end but I produced two differing specimens for her approval. The first was a straightforward 'To whom it may concern . . .' appeal, written on Curtis Brown writing paper. The other was something over which my secretary and I took a lot of loving care. We bought some mock vellum, lots of red ribbon and a good deal of sealing wax and, in italic script, wrote an appeal for assistance which started, 'Hear ye, hear ye, hear ye . . .'

Anya was delighted with both our efforts and departed on a trip which took her, amongst other places, to South Shields where, in a public library, she was touched to see a portrait of her father. The librarian was equally delighted to meet Thompson Seton's famous daughter and the encounter was to have a sequel some years later. After South Shields, her itinerary took her to ruined Rievaulx Abbey where there was a notice prominently displayed on the gate announcing that the next public opening day was the following one. Anya, of course, was not a bit deterred by such a setback and, after a little exploration, she noticed a nearby cottage where a man in shirt-sleeves was mowing the lawn. Having approached him she discovered that he was in charge of the monument. In vain she appealed for the key; in vain she explained she had to return to London that night and that it was important for her research that she had access to the ruin. All her pleadings met with a blank Yorkshire refusal. At which point Anya decided to play her last card. She delved in her briefcase and produced the much beribboned parchment. The man read it slowly and carefully. 'Just a moment, madam,' he said, 'whilst I go and change into my guide's uniform.'

Later, when Anya was writing *Devil's Water*, a story set in Northumberland, she received a letter from the civic authorities of South Shields. Would she be interested, it asked, in becoming a freeman of the city? Anya was naturally flattered and delighted at this honour to herself and retrospective honour to her father and, after a further exchange of letters, discovered she had to present herself sharply at eleven o'clock at the South Shields Town Hall. Dorothy, Anya and I had a little discussion about the implications of the hour and what she should wear and decided that probably there would be a lengthy drink session, doubtless with speeches, preceding an early lunch. Anya arrived on the hour as instructed and a glass of sherry was pressed into her hand. Evidently the occasion was going according to plan. At twelve o'clock she was tapped on the shoulder. 'It's time you were going, Miss Seton,' said an official. 'Aren't I being offered any lunch?' asked Anya in surprise. 'No,' he said sternly. 'Lunch is only for first-class freemen.' 'What am I?' asked Anya. 'Why, you're a third-class freeman,' she was told. The curiosity of a first-class novelist consumed Anya. 'And do third-class freemen have *any* privileges?' she asked. 'Oh, indeed, you can graze a pig on the town moor – but of course you provide the animal at your expense.' Anya has achieved great success and many honours but the one she cherishes most is being a third-class freeman of South Shields.

I was fortunate, on this first visit, to be present in New York when Ray Hutchinson's new book, *Elephant and Castle*, was made a single selection of the prestigious Literary Guild. Many people still regard R. C. Hutchinson as one of the most distinguished of contemporary English writers although nowadays he is sadly neglected, but this was his first enormous financial success, and his publishers, Farrar and Rinehart, flew him over to publicize the book. Ray had never been in New York before and he was bewitched by everything he saw. Stanley Rinehart, delighted at his enthusiasm, asked what especially he would like to do during his stay in the city. 'See a baseball game, and see the Twentieth Century,' said Ray. The Twentieth Century was the crack express which, in those days, made the daily journey to Chicago. Angus once travelled on it before the last war and at that time they handed out to every passenger a dollar for every minute they were late into Chicago. On this occasion Angus was sitting in the observation car, reflecting on life, when he felt a bump and, looking out, saw a dead man on the line. The train did not even slow down.

'Aren't we going to stop?' Angus asked the barman. 'Stop?' said the barman. 'What's the good of stopping? You can't bring the guy to life again and there are six hundred passengers travelling on this train.'

Anyone interested in trains, when trains were trains, would of course share Ray's wish to see such a glamorous express and, to Ray's delight, a reception was arranged for him in its bar whilst it was standing in Grand Central Station.

On the subsequent Saturday his other wish was fulfilled and we all repaired to Ebetts Field to see the Brooklyn Dodgers and the great Pee-wee Rees. Ray, by this time, was in a frenzy of enthusiasm over his trip and every subtlety of the game had to be explained to him in detail. Whilst the niceties of a 'homer' were being elucidated there was an almighty swipe from the batter, the ball soared into the air, out of the playing area, up into the stands and down into the hands of Ray. Afterwards it was autographed by the team and the success of Ray's New York visit was complete. I believe the autographed ball remained on his mantelpiece until his death.

It was on this visit that I first met Elliott Macrae, then head of the publishing firm of E. P. Dutton which we represented in London. I had a double reason for wanting to make his acquaintance as it was to his father that I had, during my Nicholson and Watson days, sold my first book. Although nowadays it is impossible to enter any expensive London restaurant without running into an American publisher on a buying spree, before the war they were as hard to encounter as garlic in an English salad. John Macrae, father of Elliott, was one of the pioneers who perceived that English books were a potential and easy source of revenue in the American market. His normal custom was to purchase a small number of sheets – the unbound pages – of the English edition and then bind them up and sell them under the Dutton imprint. By this method he acquired in the twenties an author who has probably made his publisher more money than any this century – A. A. Milne, the author of *Winnie the Pooh*, *The House at Pooh Corner* and other titles as familiar in remote parts of the world as they are to hundreds of thousands of English and American children.

On one of John Macrae's buying trips he called in at my office and I gave him proofs of Evan John's great historical novel, *Crippled Splendour*. I was doubly delighted when Macrae acquired the American rights because I had been subjected to a certain amount of teasing by my colleagues in insisting that we publish the book. Evan John, a poetic personality both in appearance and character, had arrived in Essex Street bearing what appeared to be an enormous laundry basket. Out of it he nervously pulled seemingly thousands of manuscript pages, all written in beautiful Italianate script and with each chapter heading exquisitely embossed with a gaily hand-painted shield. It was the fictionalized life of James I and I am happy to recall that it made a reasonable amount of money for a first novelist who later went on to greater triumphs before a premature death cut off what was undoubtedly a major talent.

Although I first met Elliott Macrae in New York it was in London that his personality flowered. From the late forties onwards Elliott became one of the best-loved Americans on the English publishing scene. He was a marvellous amalgam of the naïve, the shrewd and the sentimental. Generous to a fault, like many of his fellow-countrymen, he was deeply distressed at the state in which he found England during his first postwar visit. Therefore, for years, long after rationing had ceased, his English friends were from time to time the recipients of great peach-fed hams, crates of tea, and truckles of cheese. Many Americans were generous but there was an element of personal involvement in the universal English distress that was peculiar to Elliott.

Perhaps it came from his Scottish birthright. He loved to boast of his Caledonian origins and one of his earliest purchases in Britain was a kilt in the Macrae plaid. I remember him wearing it for the first time. He became a widely travelled man, prepared to journey to the most unlikely quarters of the globe on the faint chance of finding a book. And where Elliott went, his camera went with him. The result of this orgy of photography was, as a rule, a public film show at the Dorchester, accompanied by lots of drink and a commentary by Elliott who delighted in his role as a lecturer. His appearance in his new kilt at one of these occasions was a ten-day wonder in the book trade.

Elliott acquired his books by instinct. I never knew him to read them before buying the American rights. I always lunched with him early in his trip and I regarded it as a very unsuccessful meeting if he had not bought at least two of my offerings by the time we had reached the coffee. He never doubted my judgement and, in turn, I saw to it that the books I sold him were right for his list. In the forties and fifties he acquired for Dutton's an astonishing list of English-based best-sellers: *Seven Years in Tibet*, *A Reed Shaken by the Wind, Arabian Sands, Annapurna, The Conquest of Everest* amongst them.

Elliott loved such books and journeying all over the world to find them. He was once travelling through the uplands of New Zealand on a sight-seeing trip with Marjorie, his wife. They overtook a push-bike ridden by a girl with a Union Jack on her knapsack. Elliott instantly stopped the car and waved her down. It transpired that she had cycled out from England. Elliott pulled out his pocket-book and presented her with a $100 note and his business card. 'Call me up when you get to New York and we'll sign a contract.' I never heard whether the book was written.

Some English publishers chose to be a little dismissive of a man who never had any pretentions about his intellectual capacities and who certainly possessed some touchingly naïve characteristics. I once took him on his first visit to the Ritz restaurant, by common consent one of the most beautiful in London. Elliott paused at the entrance to admire the view of Green Park seen through the great crystal chandeliers. 'Look at that, Marjorie,' he said to his wife. 'It's just like the *Queen Mary*.'

But you could not but succumb to the warmth and charm and friendliness of his personality. Elliott would have had no use for the present publishing world of computers and data banks and accountants.

If my trip to America in 1948 opened many doors to future relationships on both a professional and personal level – and one of the charms of the book trade is that they so often overlap – my return in 1950 with Dorothy was of a different order. Americans respond to enthusiasm and, even more, they respond to enthusiasm from young and very pretty girls. Dorothy, never one to play down her enthusiasm, was bowled over by New York and our American friends fell over backwards in vying with each other to give her whatever New York had to offer. At the time

the great postwar era of the American musical was in full
flood and had reached its high tide with the production of *South
Pacific*. In London one's friends were divided between those who
possessed a recording of the show and those who didn't. There
was a strict embargo on the playing of the music in England
pending the production in London and there was a lively trade in
smuggled records. Lucky owners found themselves possessed of
a temporary social status which greatly elevated them amongst
their friends. In New York there was a waiting list of six months
for seats at the box office. Nothing in theatrical history could
compete with its success or the triumph of its star, Mary
Martin.

Well, naturally, Dorothy was asked what theatres she would
like to go to. And naturally Dorothy – not, I suspect without a
touch of wickedness – said what a pity there was no chance of
getting into *South Pacific*. It was sufficient! Not for nothing is
America a matriarchal society. Not for nothing are Americans
dynamic and successful. Did not somebody have a friend who
knew Oscar Hammerstein? Were there not such things as house-
seats? Should not the visiting English have a chance of seeing the
best of the contemporary American theatre? John Farrar, after
goodness knows what machinations, eventually got us seats and
Dorothy and I, sick with excitement, took ourselves off to see
Mary Martin in a theatre where the atmosphere was electric.
As we opened the programme a slip of paper fell out. It announced
that the star was indisposed and her part would be played that
night by a Miss Dolores Gray. I think we were both near tears.
It is only fair to say that Miss Gray, who was soon to captivate
London in the lead of *Annie Get Your Gun* was a wholly ravishing
alternative and the show appeared to lose nothing by the
absence of the star.

There was a sequel. In due course Mary Martin came to
London with *South Pacific* and, to assuage Dorothy's earlier dis-
appointment, I, too, pulled strings and procured tickets – also
after huge difficulty – for the first night. At the time Dorothy
was pregnant and we decided to have a light meal of oysters

before the performance. Sad to tell, although Miss Martin was certainly playing that night, we didn't manage to see much of her. Most of the time we drove round and round the deserted streets of Covent Garden with Dorothy very sick out of the car window. She has never eaten an oyster since.

What pleasure we got from that great series of American musicals that ran through the immediate postwar decades! I still remember the dismay I felt at the prospect of a visit to *West Side Story* – 'Romeo and Juliet in a New York tenement', was my host's deliberately off-putting description. I still recall the actuality of Leonard Bernstein's music, Stephen Sondheim's lyrics and the vitality of a production which was like a repeated series of electric shocks. There was the visit, later in the sixties, with Elaine and John Steinbeck, to the all-black production of *Hello, Dolly* which I had previously seen twice in London, without much enthusiasm, in spite of Mary Martin in the lead. But a black performance has something which, in a musical, no white players can reproduce and the coloured cast, headed by the ravishing Pearl Bailey, had the entire theatre on its feet in a standing ovation. Perhaps the grass is always greener in another man's field, but there is a vibrancy about theatre-going in New York which seems absent from Shaftesbury Avenue. It's equally true that nowadays the lights of Broadway are not so bright as they once were and it's no added attraction to find that it's hard to get to the theatre, since one is advised not to walk for fear of being mugged, taxis are at a premium and somehow it always seems to be raining.

It was around this time that Dorothy and I first became friendly with Ruth McKenney and her husband Richard Bransten. Ruth was a plump, bouncing, brash Irish girl who had found instant fame and fortune by writing a book called *My Sister Eileen*. Subsequently, as happened to Christopher Isherwood's *Sally Bowles*, it reappeared in successive versions, starting as a play, becoming a film, then being converted into a musical which, in turn, became another movie. Ruth, in the meantime, moved to

Hollywood where she became a successful scriptwriter and where nothing would, in all likelihood, have interfered with the equanimity of their prosperous lives were it not for the fact that Richard, scion of the owner of a big grocery chain, was editor of the Marxist magazine, *New Masses*. Both he and Ruth were quite open in their advocacy of communism. The political climate of America has never been conducive to the promotion of such beliefs and the cold war, which was to lead into the era of Senator McCarthy, was an ugly backdrop to those who promoted them. In due course the Branstens decided the English climate was more sympathetic to their views and they bought a house in Chelsea and moved in with their family.

Whether the immediate postwar literary world was particularly thin-blooded or whether Ruth's irrepressible Irish-American self-confidence bulldozed everything before her, there is no doubt that she quickly became a popular dinner-party guest. Well-loved as they both quickly became, there was the added pleasure for the host and hostess that, apart from pouring out the wine and serving up the food, no further effort to entertain their guests was necessary. It is true that occasionally, around midnight, one sometimes saw a slightly hunted look at the table as Ruth remorselessly talked on. Richard, a gentle intellectual who worked at that time for Rupert Hart-Davis, was happy to let his adored wife make the social running. Their new life seemed indisputably a success.

But the cold war was not so easy to escape. Soon Senator McCarthy's ugly image began to intrude into every conversation. As at the time of the Spanish Civil War, friends started avoiding friends. It was a time for choosing sides. The Branstens, to their eternal credit, returned to America, Richard to become an editor in a publishing house, Ruth to continue writing, the children to go to American schools.

But it did not work. How could it? Dorothy and I spent a weekend at their modest house in Westport and it was obvious that the tolerance they had encountered in London did not extend to their new circle. Richard joked about their three-year-old car which he maintained the town sneeringly considered obsolescent, the second-hand fridge and the lack of a freezer. At school the children were excluded by their fellows. But the jokes sounded flat and it was no surprise when we heard the Branstens were once more to escape to London.

But this time the escape didn't work. Something had changed. Ruth had been commissioned to write a huge novel for a huge sum. The pages poured out of her typewriter but she was far too professional not to know that they were rubbish. Richard returned to publishing, but his creative vigour had gone. The dinner parties ceased, their friends were rebuffed. We managed to keep in touch and one day Ruth rang me up. 'Isn't it wonderful,' she said with something of her old enthusiasm. 'Richard and I have talked things through and everything is going to be all right. We're through this blackness. Tomorrow's my birthday and Richard's taking me out to celebrate.'

The next day Richard took his life.

We saw Ruth often after that and quite soon the novelist's creative gifts got transferred into real-life fantasies. She became paranoid and one day, unexpectedly, we heard she had gone to live in Rome. From there, from time to time, I was the recipient of emotional late night calls, but no one was able to persuade her to seek medical care. And then Dorothy and I saw her for the last time.

We were in Venice one summer when, coincidentally, the film festival was taking place. One night, pretty late, we were walking home to our hotel through St Mark's Square. Suddenly, outside Florian's, we saw a familiar figure. It was Ruth, sitting at a table with her daughter, Eileen. I bent down, said hello and kissed her. Ruth looked up, got up from the table and promptly fainted. Even at that late hour we were soon the centre of a group of excited Italians. Soon a glass of *grappa* restored Ruth to something approaching her old vitality whilst she regaled us with macabre stories of persecution by the police and secret services of three countries in whose pay she found most of her erstwhile friends.

'What are you doing in Venice?' we asked.

'I want to see Dilys Powell,' she said. 'If I sit here long enough I'm bound to find her.'

'And how long have you been sitting?' I asked.

'Three days so far.'

Dilys Powell in those days was the film critic of the *Sunday Times* and therefore likely to be in Venice for the festival. I never discovered what role Ruth expected her to play in this last pathetic tragedy, for she died soon after.

Through Elliott Macrae, at the time his American publisher, I first met Gore Vidal who, in 1948, had just published his first novel *Williwaw* which had as a background the war in the Pacific. Soon he was to write *The City and the Pillar*, one of the first novels with a homosexual theme to find wide acceptance.

Gore is one of the most engaging men I have known. He frightens me to death. I have only met one other who combined his startling good looks with his massive creative intelligence and devastating wit, and that was Noel Coward. In the presence of both I suffer, or suffered, from a raging feeling of inadequacy. My inferiority was not helped in the case of my first meeting with Noel Coward by being invited by him in his suite in the Savoy Hotel to sit in a chair which immediately collapsed. Coward was his charming, urbane self in helping me to my feet, but the incident did not help to restore my self-confidence. I have never been flat on the floor in front of Gore but I have often felt that the happening was imminent.

Gore has a perfectly efficient hard-working American agent who looks after the bulk of his numerous activities. There is no conceivable reason why he should continue his relationship with me. I think he does so because he feels there is a certain olde worlde charm about dealing with a firm which has been established for nearly a century. He uses us, with infinite courtesy, primarily in the capacity of a butler or a valet or, occasionally, as a banker. At his request we send flowers to famous actresses on their opening nights, we order another dozen pairs of shoes from Peal's, we settle £500 bills for books ordered from Heywood Hill.

Occasionally I swap inadequate gossip with him in his suite at the Connaught. At no point am I asked to carry out more than the perfunctory duties of a literary agent. I am very fond of Gore. I think he is fond of me. I find the relationship endearing – if a little frightening.

During the war, paper, like most other commodities, was rationed. Books, because of the black-out and a lack of competing entertainment, were in enormous demand. Most publishers simply did not have a sufficient supply of paper to print as many copies as they knew they could sell. Very long books, with their extravagant demand for the basic raw material were, therefore, apt to be looked on with disfavour. It was for this reason that *Forever Amber*, which became a huge runaway American best-seller, for some time failed to find an English publisher. There was no difficulty in recognizing the saleability of this long historical novel which was also, by the standards of the day, regarded as being slightly salacious. Nor was its saleability in any way lessened by its immensely photogenic author, the very beautiful Kathleen Winsor.

Having been declined by a number of the more established publishers on the grounds of length, it was sent to a relatively new firm, Macdonald. Macdonald had been founded shortly after the outbreak of war by the large and prosperous firm of printers, Purnells, now part of the BPC Group. Many printers, owing to the eccentricities of the rationing law, had more paper than they needed. This anomaly arose because printers print, publish and distribute a wide range of catalogues, leaflets, posters and the like. As such, under wartime licensing they were entitled to their ration of paper. But, of course, many of its uses had disappeared with the war. Purnells sensibly decided that part of their allocation could profitably be used in publishing. Thus the firm of Macdonald came into existence. I never knew why the name was chosen but I have heard it said that it was called after their London representative.

Macdonald, with tons of paper to spare, were offered the widely admired plum *Forever Amber*, and were wholly undeterred by its length. They realized it was exactly the potential best-sellers every new publisher prays for – although statistics suggest their prayers are seldom answered. They were not disappointed. The book caught the mood of a war-weary public, starved of romance and glamour, and sold in hundreds of thousands. Everyone was delighted.

Some few years later the glamorous Kathleen Winsor decided to pay her first visit to London. I rang up the editor at Macdonald's – I think his name was Thompson – and suggested that we had better co-ordinate our entertainment during her stay. There seemed to be a noticeable lack of enthusiasm at the other end of the telephone, but I promised to keep him in touch with her arrangements. In due course she arrived and all that I need to say is that her charm and likeability entirely matched her stunning looks. Perhaps her historical sense sometimes led her astray – as had been said by some unkindly critics of the book – because I remember her commenting with admiration on the 'Tudor' houses she noticed on the road in from London airport. Dorothy and I had enormous fun in showing her the sights. She was a most appreciative guest. In the meantime there was total silence from Mr Thompson.

Eventually, after four days, Kathleen modestly suggested that it really might be a good idea if she were to meet her publisher.

'Now look here, Mr Thompson,' I said severely. 'You've really got to do something about meeting this girl.'

Mr Thompson, sad that the problem had not magically disappeared, arranged a lunch with her at the Café Royal. I was eating a sandwich in my office when my telephone rang. It was an agitated Kathleen ringing from the restaurant.

'Graham,' she said in some irritation, 'you've got to get me away from this guy, whatever my contract says. He started by offering me a drink. I said I didn't drink till evening. He thought I was lying. "Go on, Miss Winsor, don't be coy. No one'll see you here. Of course you must have a drink." He offered me a cigarette. I said I didn't smoke. "Go on," he said. "Don't be coy. You don't have to pretend with me. Do have a cigarette." I can't think what his next move will be after lunch. I suspect he's identifying me with the heroine of my book.'

There are more ways of losing an author than not selling their books. I moved Kathleen Winsor to Peter Davies. Nicholas, one of the Davies brothers who jointly inspired Barrie's Peter Pan – had a passion for, and encyclopaedic knowledge of, jazz. Any spare hour when he was in New York he could be discovered in Eddie Condon's club blowing a trumpet. He was also a great fisherman. It was therefore wholly in accordance with the general dottiness of the book trade that Peter Davies Ltd, made most of their money publishing books in which neither of the brothers appeared to have any particular interest, namely, of popular religion. Their first success in this field came from publishing the great religious novels of Lloyd Douglas. Few critics would award them any marks for literary merit, but they certainly caught the taste of the public. When, therefore, I was asked to find an English publisher for *A Man Called Peter*, I immediately thought of Nico.

A Man Called Peter was written by a Scotswoman, Catherine Marshall, and told the story of her husband's ministry in Washington. In America it was a runaway best-seller where its approach to religion on a very popular fundamentalist base appeared to have caught the taste of the public. In Great Britain it seemed to me to have a very limited appeal although the sincerity of the writing and the message it conveyed were there for all to see.

Nico read it and after a little returned it to me with a letter which said, 'I was very moved by the book. I would have liked to publish it. But I can't see a market for it in this country.' Accordingly, I sent it on its rounds and it was seen and rejected for the same reason by half a dozen of the most likely publishers. At this point about a year had elapsed since the book had been originally submitted to Peter Davies. Then, one day, my telephone rang. It was Nico.

'Have you sold that book by Catherine Marshall that you offered me months ago?'

I told him what had happened.

'Well,' said Nico, 'I'm going to make you a modest offer for it. As I haven't been able to put it out of my mind after six months, there must be something quite a bit special about it.'

Peter Davies published *A Man Called Peter* to a deafening silence. There were virtually no reviews, there was scarcely any advertising, sales after six months were derisory. During the next six months I happened to notice that sales had trebled, admittedly from a very low base. And then there arrived in London a film based on the book. It opened at the Empire, Leicester Square and was so savagely attacked by the critics that it was taken off after three disastrous days – something hitherto unknown in the history of a theatre where a week was the minimum run.

During the next six months Peter Davies reported sales which had quadrupled. And then suddenly, no one knows why, an avalanche started. Where previously it had sold in tens a month it now started to sell in hundreds, with the pace quickening month by month. In only a matter of two or three years, Nico's modest hunch was into a six-figure sale and is still selling steadily twenty years later. As they would doubtless say in Hollywood, 'That's book business.'

CHAPTER SEVEN

During most of my early years in the book trade Stanley Unwin was the doyen of publishing. He died in his eighties still at his desk, his eightieth birthday having been celebrated by the attendance at the Stationers' Hall of all the high brass of the book trade anxious to pay homage to this distinguished figure. This occasion, I recollect, differed from an earlier Allen and Unwin function which I attended, in that alcoholic drink was provided. This was in contrast to the launching party for the book *Kon-Tiki*, probably the greatest success in the firm's history until it was supplanted by the Tolkien books which became an all-pervading cult. On that occasion only tea and cakes were served before the speeches and subsequent showing of the film of the expedition. Consequently there were many long faces, not solely amongst the free-loaders of Fleet Street, and if the book later took off under its own momentum, the promotional party could not be rated a success.

Teetotalism was an important factor in Unwin's life. At one time I was a fellow member of the Reform. Angus who, in many ways, resembled Unwin in background and outlook, knew him a little and, although I was of a different generation, when, from time to time, we met casually in the Club, he would suggest that we lunched together. Although I regard drink as one of the great pleasures of life I am perfectly able to do without it but, because both Angus and Unwin sought to impose their views, I felt it incumbent on me to take a modest stand. So before lunch I made a point of ordering an aperitif. Unwin would shake his head at the sight of the demon drink. 'How your father would suffer if he saw you drinking that,' he would say.

Unwin was one of the last of the Victorians, a breed which made England commercially great and is now derided by a generation which has discarded its values without having any precise idea with what to replace them. Short in stature, with a little goatee beard, his tie encircled by a ring, his accent clipped, his gait sharp and agile, he was a Liberal and a Nonconformist who believed, along with his generation, in the virtues of hard work. He had little sympathy for those whose standards were softer than his own or who felt the world owed them a living. Long after most publishers had reverted to a five-day week Allen and Unwin were working on Saturday mornings. His journey to the office – naturally, of course, Unwin walked – took him along Great Russell Street and past the office of Hamish Hamilton. One Saturday he noticed that Hamilton's was on fire. He hurried to the telephone. 'Mr Hamilton, I fear your office is on fire.' Then he paused for a moment, timing the tagline. 'What a pity you, too, aren't open on Saturdays.'

Unwin must have been a fairly rich man and towards the end of his life he built himself a well-appointed house in Hampstead which contained, as well as many electronic gadgets, its own tennis court. He continued to play tennis right through his seventies and to celebrate the new court he invited Billy Collins, who had played at Wimbledon and was a regular opponent, up for the inaugural game. Billy invited Laurence Meynell as his partner and the foursome knocked up for some time with a set of old balls.

'Well, I think we might start now,' said Unwin in his precise tones. 'Unwrap some new balls from that box, will you, Laurie.'

Laurence started to strip off the tissue paper, watched by Unwin from the other side of the net. When three were exposed from their wrapping there came a further instruction. 'I think they'll do for the moment.'

Unwin kept a tight control on every aspect of his business including personally opening all the firm's post. A very active member of the Publishers Association, concerning himself with every aspect of book trade politics, he became the voice of the book trade on nearly all official matters in dealing with the Government. He, more than anybody, persuaded the Government not to impose a purchase tax on books during the war. In addition he became a familiar sight to booksellers in remote and inaccessible corners of the world. Although Billy Collins was to catch him up fast he was the first to explore on a personal level the huge potential of overseas trade.

There was a generation of younger men who worked with him in the business and who must sometimes have had their eye on the highest position, who must have wondered whether the old boy was immortal. But when Unwin died a world died with him.

If Unwin was the doyen of publishing Billy Collins was, indisputably, the most commercially successful publisher. For this he was naturally not forgiven by his contemporaries who envied Billy's ruthless efficiency without being able to emulate it. Much snide comment passed about his piratical raids on the lists of other publishers, but the plain fact was that many writers were attracted to an imprint where the professional efficiency of the operation tended to earn the writer a substantially larger income than he was, in all probability, likely to achieve elsewhere. This skill was not come by lightly. Although Billy was an accomplished sportsman at tennis, cricket and swimming, he lived only for publishing. I doubt whether his mind was ever far from his publishing business or that he had many friends who could not contribute to it. In latter years, having built up a useful support team in London, he increasingly travelled the world and was to be seen as often as Unwin in remote bookshops situated in pleasurable quarters of the world. He was one of the first to recognize the importance of owning overseas offices in the build-up of export business. Collins's publishing operation, for instance, in Australia, is a great deal bigger than many well-regarded English imprints and their other overseas companies are of comparable importance.

Collins, like all other firms, occasionally rejected a book which subsequently made some lucky publisher a fortune. There is a story told about *Elsa the Lion* which, I suspect, is at least partially true. It concerns the purchase of the Harvill Press as an outlet for the promotion of Roman Catholic books shortly after Pierre Collins, Billy's wife, had become a convert to the faith. The Harvill Press was, at the time, a small, distinguished imprint run by two ladies, Manya Harari, a Russian married to an Egyptian banker, and Marjorie Villiers. The firm was purchased by Collins for, I believe, a very modest sum, and amongst their acquisitions Collins discovered that they had bought the rights to publish *Dr Zhivago* and *The Leopard*, both of which became international best-sellers. Also on the list was a book they had earlier seen and declined called *Elsa the Lion*.

The history of *Elsa the Lion*, soon to become the biggest best-seller of them all, was not an unusual one. Written in exceedingly bad English and accompanied by a number of not especially distinguished photographs of lions, it had been submitted to a large number of publishers and agents. It had been declined by Collins as, sadly, it had also been declined by Curtis Brown. It was not really a very attractive proposition. Finally it reached the desk of Marjorie Villiers at the Harvill Press. The firm had recently published, with modest success, another animal photo-graphic book by the photographer Ylla, and Mrs Villiers felt that properly edited there were possibilities in *Elsa the Lion* as a successor. The author, Joy Adamson, agreed to its re-editing and some re-writing and the first edition appeared under the Harvill Press imprint at about the time of the purchase by Collins. It was an instant success. The second impression soon appeared, this time under the joint imprint of the Harvill Press and William Collins. The third impression followed and this time the imprint was William Collins and the Harvill Press. The remaining nine hundred and ninety-nine editions appeared under the imprint of William Collins only. Billy had once more got his money back.

There is a story about Billy, doubtless apocryphal, which could serve as his epitaph. One of his very famous novelists was reported to him as having died of a sudden heart attack. 'How could he do that to us after all we've done for him?' said Billy.

I never knew Harold Macmillan in his publishing capacity although, for a number of years, I had the pleasure of acting, from time to time, as his literary agent, as I did for two other prime ministers. For some reason I have always felt for Mr Macmillan a great affection such as I rarely accord to my political masters and I always recall with pleasure that marvellous face which resembles nothing so much as a St Bernard which has had too much port for dinner. As a matter of fact, my daughter Sophie made his acquaintance before I did. Sophie was a friend of Louise Amery, Mr Macmillan's granddaughter, and on one occasion when she was about eight and Mr Macmillan was still the prime minister she was invited down to Birch Grove for the weekend. At one moment, she was sitting alone reading in the library when Mr Macmillan entered. He peered at her tall slender form crowned by cropped hair, as was the fashion at the time, and enquired, 'Tell me, which of my grandsons are you?'

I remember a reception at the Savoy given by his publishers to celebrate the last volume of his memoirs. On the platform were three prime ministers: Edward Heath (then incumbent), Harold Wilson and Harold Macmillan. Mr Heath spoke for some two or three minutes, rather gracelessly, about his pleasure in serving Mr Macmillan when he was his chief whip. Mr Wilson followed and, for a quarter of an hour, spoke warmly and with obvious affection emphasizing an admiration for the guest of the evening. Then Mr Macmillan got up to reply, holding in his hand notes to which he never needed to refer. He spoke of Mr Wilson and his premiership with some degree of affection. One felt that the two ex-prime ministers each respected the prowess of the other as professional parliamentary gladiators. Then Mr Macmillan turned to Mr Heath and, for a sentence or two, referred to their past association. 'I shall always be grateful,' said Mr Macmillan, and here he paused and screwed up his eyes and raised his notes and peered at them short-sightedly before bringing them up to the light the better to see what he had written. 'I shall always be grateful,' he repeated, 'for Mr Heath's great loyalty.' The packed audience exploded!

Once, after I had been discussing with him some professional matter, he showed me to the lift in his office. It was the occasion of one of the miners' strikes which was then paralysing the country. 'What, sir, do you think of the miners?' I asked, to make conversation. 'The miners,' replied Mr Macmillan, dead-pan, 'are a fine body of men. They are like the aristocracy, they're only interested in drink, sex and gambling.'

A very different figure was Walter Hutchinson whose hobby was the collecting of publishing imprints. Either immediately preceding the war or shortly after it, he bought, amongst others, Rider, Dennis Archer, Jarrolds, Hurst and Blackett, Stanley Paul, Arrowsmith, John Long, Rich and Cowan and Popular Dogs. As Hutchinson had some of the characteristics of megalomania it is possible that he purchased these largely worthless companies purely in a mood of magpie acquisition. There was also a theory, commonly advanced at the time, that cross-fertilization between the associated companies gave a flexibility to the balance sheets which was not necessarily supported by the underlying assets. During the first great war-time fire raid on London, Hutchinson's warehouse in Paternoster Row near St Paul's Cathedral was completely destroyed. It contained two million pounds' worth of over-valued stock and some unkind critics of the company were heard to express the view that the bomb had certainly fallen with the proprietor's, if not with God's, blessing. However, whatever the reason – and certainly the war was a godsend to Hutchinson as to so many other publishers – the ramshackle empire held together until, under the management of Robert Lusty, rationalization took place and it was formed into the prosperous and distinguished group which is much admired today.

Of course, the importance of these separate imprints should not be over-emphasized. In each, Hutchinson appointed a manager, miserably underpaid, but someone glad of even a pittance in an era of high unemployment, who was in nominal charge of the editorial functions of the company, sometimes of two companies. The manager comprised the entire staff of each imprint. As a back-up there were the servicing departments which provided secretarial, production, sales and promotional facilities. As every purchase of a book, its jacket, blurb and advertising appropriation had to be approved by Mr Walter (as Hutchinson was generally called), the back-log and delay in administration would have done credit to the Civil Service. It is true that some of the lists, especially the main imprint, contained the names of a number of distinguished authors. But, nevertheless, a proportion of Hutchinson's books at least were being published for the remainder market. The method was as follows.

A book would be published which was probably called something like, *My Travels by Tram through Rainy Patagonia*. The published price would be twenty-one shillings and a few hundreds might, with luck, be sold to the libraries and through export. Then, a few months later, the price would be slashed to five shillings and a garish band drawing attention to this great bargain would be put round the jacket. Of course the book had been costed originally to show a profit at the lower price.

Hutchinson was a collector of sporting pictures of which he had perhaps the finest collection in private hands. In order to show them off in a suitable setting he bought the elegant stately home, Derby House, which lies in a cul-de-sac off Oxford Street. Here the ground floor salons were to house the collection whilst the rest of the house would contain the staff of the office. No one dared to object that the attic bedrooms, designed for servants, were hardly suited for adoption as twentieth-century offices. Nor was the house sufficiently large to accommodate the whole staff. Every alternative was considered but there was no way of fitting in a final eleven bodies. Hutchinson was approached for his advice. 'Sack them,' he said.

I like to recall the episode of the curator. Once the pictures had been assembled Hutchinson was able to arrange through the new curator, who had met Queen Mary in a previous occupation, that Her Majesty would officially open the exhibition. Hutchinson, who was believed to be angling for a title, looked forward to the occasion. The reception party lined up, Mr and Mrs Hutchinson to the front, the curator three steps to the rear. Queen Mary descended from her car, swept past Hutchinson, greeted the curator and insisted he accompany her round the gallery.

War between Hutchinson and the curator was instantly declared. The curator lived in a flat in the building and stoutly refused to listen to any suggestions that he should vacate it. Hutchinson then gave instructions that his mail be impounded. Still the curator refused to be discountenanced. After all, immediately after the war, a job was a job. One was not then, as now, paid huge sums in severance pay following dismissal. So Hutchinson dismissed him for incompetence and the other directors of the company were ordered to approve this decision at board level. Peter Kimber, one of the directors, refused to support any such resolution as there was not the slightest evidence to suggest that the curator was in any way incompetent. Peter's stand infuriated Hutchinson who was not used to insubordination and, although he was easily the most experienced and senior editor in the group, he too found himself dismissed. Peter sued Hutchinson for wrongful dismissal, received heavy damages and with them started his own distinguished imprint, William Kimber.

Another bizarre figure from about the same period was John Holroyd-Reece, which patronym was corrupted from the original Teutonic Reisz. His mother was English but taught in a Montessori school in Holland. John himself was educated at Repton whose Puritan disciplines – I speak as an old Reptonian of only a slightly later period – were an odd springboard for a figure who quickly developed the physical characteristics of a Peter Ustinov or a George Weidenfeld. All three men could only have sprung from mainland Europe and all have an aura of physical well-being which appears to arise from far too great an indulgence in goose liver and other delicacies which originate in the south-east corner of France. John spent his early days in publishing selling books for Ernest Benn, an occupation he shared at the time with Victor Gollancz, and Douglas Jerrold, who later ran Eyre and Spottiswoode. This appears to be a promising springboard for future giants of publishing because Jonathan Cape was also, during this period, a traveller for Gerald Duckworth. However, like the other two men, Holroyd-Reece had no intention of continuing for long to make money for other men. Very soon he was off to Paris where he quickly made, and spent, a small fortune selling art books from an *atelier* on the left bank. Then he decided to challenge the might of Tauchnitz who, at the time, had a monopoly on the continent of Europe in producing in the English language, and in a handsome and reasonably priced form, best-selling English and American writers. Every traveller in those leisured days would expect to pick up in a local bookshop or on a railway bookstall a sufficiency of reading matter under the Tauchnitz imprint to suit his needs whilst on holiday. The books, of course, pre-dated the arrival of Penguin and the mass-market paperback. They were published with German thoroughness and they were immensely successful. Holroyd-Reece, backed, it was said, by Nazi Government funds, decided to challenge the Tauchnitz predominance and he founded a rival series under a new imprint, Albatross books. It was not long before Albatross had the satisfaction of absorbing Tauchnitz although it, too, succumbed after the war when Europe became open to the full onslaught of British-American mass paperback imprints.

It was just before the outbreak of war that John first came into my life. He arrived at Paternoster Row with a proposition that Nicholson and Watson and Albatross should use their joint resources to form a new joint hardback/paperback imprint. The suggestion was way ahead of its time although, twenty years later, such an arrangement was a commonplace. However, Nicholson and Watson were still struggling with profitability after losing a large proportion of their capital, the war was obviously imminent and Angus, perhaps wisely, refused to dip any deeper into his pockets.

Initially I was glad about this decision. There are few men I have distrusted on sight more than I did John Holroyd-Reece. His huge fleshy jowls and triple chin, the tiny, piggy eyes, his thick fat lips from which always hung a French cigarette on which John contrived to retain at least an inch of ash, his bulging neck pressing down over his collar, all added up to a man whom I would not readily trust if he were to tell me the weather forecast. John, always sensitive to the reactions of his audience, quickly realized this and, because it suited his book, he started to talk me into a change of mind. And John was, I suppose, one of the most engaging talkers I have ever listened to. Whether this contributed in any way to his notorious sexual charm I cannot say, but I soon found him irresistible.

He would talk, and then he would talk and then he would talk again. And when he had finished talking he would talk some more. And whilst he talked he would pace up and down the room, a half smile on his lips, watching his effect on you. And the effect, in general, was considerable. Against every instinct one would succumb. He had a marvellous café-society knowledge of contemporary life. He knew everyone and had done everything. If he was giving you a lot of horse manure at least you knew it was straight from the horse's mouth or wherever.

You would mention a forthcoming visit to Rome.

'In Rome,' said John, 'you buy silk pyjamas. The shop is off the Via Veneto, second turning on the left, past the café Veneto, number 33, second floor up. Ask for Luigi and mention my name. And be sure the silk is Burmese and not Thai.'

You are about to set out for a visit to America.

'You must especially go to Tiffany's. It's a little restaurant on 8th and 23rd. Rather a tough district so take a taxi. Don't be put off by the entrance. Mention me to Harry and ask for his blue-fish with the special curry sauce. But don't go on Wednesday because the chef has the night off.'

Of course I found this sort of chat irresistible, although I also found it infuriating that he was nearly always right. The Burmese silk pyjamas were a dream, and Harry's sauce a poem.

After the outbreak of war the negotiations with Nicholson and Watson continued in a desultory fashion, mainly, I think, because John's association with the company, which had then developed into a more formal arrangement, was then his main form of financial support. As evidence as to how far my original mistrust had been dissipated, my sister Diana and I loaned him our flat, rent free, for the remainder of the lease since neither of us, for differing reasons, had any further use for it. I disappeared abroad to the desert where the only intrusion of Holroyd-Reece in a rather different sort of campaign came with a long-delayed letter from Diana, expressing some anxiety about him based on local London gossip which she thought might involve her (if not others) as he was living in our flat. In an equally delayed letter I advised her to approach Scotland Yard to express her alarm and, some months later, I heard that she had done so and been assured that they knew all about John Holroyd-Reece and that she need have no worry. It was possible to put any interpretation on this statement that one fancied.

And then, shortly after the end of the war he disappeared from sight. There were reports from Milan that he was running a dancing school. Then rumours circulated about his buying a castle in Kent. Later a small press report gave news of some entanglement with the police when he arrived in England unannounced in a small aeroplane at a remote airfield. And then, a few years later, his death was reported. I have always felt that some author should emulate A. J. A. Symons whose brilliant *Quest for Corvo* set a new fashion in investigative biography. *Quest for Holroyd-Reece* might throw a little light into the dark corners of the life of this mysterious man.

CHAPTER EIGHT

THE position of an agent is rather akin to that of the popular French sex symbol Alfonse – lucky Alfonse who was always in the middle. For the moment however let us leave Alfonse's sex life to the imagination and concentrate instead on his hunting proclivities. One recalls the tweeded Englishman with his Purdy guns, invited to shoot over Alfonse's estate. A rabbit appears at their feet. The Englishman raises his gun. 'Do not shoot,' says Alfonse. 'That is Gaston. We never shoot at Gaston.' They walk on and another rabbit rises from the stubble. 'Blaze away,' shouts Alfonse. 'That is Philippe; we always shoot at Philippe.'

With the agent in the favoured position of being always in the middle, his friends tend to be equally divided between publishers and authors. Dorothy and I have been blessed with a close circle of friends from both worlds and there is probably no other professional activity which brings one into contact with so many agreeable people. I suppose that age tends to diminish, and youth to exaggerate the contemporary scene, thus the greatest publishing figures of all seem to me to belong to the time when I was young.

There was an eruption of new publishers in the twenties which saw the birth, amongst others, of the great firms of Faber and Faber, Hamish Hamilton, Jonathan Cape and Victor Gollancz. The wretched decade which followed and which led up to the Second World War manifested no shortage of money and the flow of rash newcomers continued with the founding of our own firm, Ivor Nicholson and Watson, which scarcely survived the war; Michael Joseph, which struggled on until it found prosperity, as did many others, with the coming of the black-out and the virtual disappearance of outside entertainment; Arthur Barker, a rich man's toy which was ultimately bought by a printer and then sold to Weidenfeld and Nicolson; Rich and Cowan, another wealthy man's plaything, which was swallowed up by the giant squid of the Hutchinson empire, and many more, unremembered, unsung. But one firm founded in the decade before the war and which was to alter the face of publishing was Penguin. But more of this later.

After the war it seems as though English-born publishers were either demoralized or hard up and, for some years, the greatest contribution to British publishing came from those whose birthright was European, but who achieved wide success amongst the idle and depressed English by a combination of hard necessity, hard work and, occasionally, a willingness, if needs be, to accept hard labour. The list is long, with Weidenfeld and Nicolson, André Deutsch, Souvenir Press and Thames and Hudson *primi inter pares*. These firms achieved their success through the personalities of the men who created them, a lesson ignored by a world where the inexorable advance to power of the accountant and the lawyer continues. One has only to look across the ocean to America to see the effect of these faceless executives controlling a business which must ultimately depend on the individuality and freedom of the men who find the books. Already there is an effort to rediscover the formula which will give personality to those huge conglomerates which now dominate the New York scene. One device, which amounts to no more than an ego trip for the editor concerned is to publish a book under his name jointly with the publisher. A John Doe book published by Jack Smith Inc. John Doe, of course, is an editor sufficiently well-regarded as to be able to retain authors more loyal to him than the firm who employs him and publishes them. But this is only a façade behind which still gather the faceless committees, the money men and the computers.

It is hard to believe that the great giants of publishing could possibly have functioned against such a background, and I especially single out the two whom I regard as the greatest publishers of my lifetime, Victor Gollancz and Allen Lane, the founder of Penguin. Victor and his wife Ruth became close friends of ours, a liking for kitchen bridge being as strong a bond as the world of books. It is impossible to write of Victor except in terms of deep and abiding love and yet, in many ways, he was an outrageous character. Under that unruly mane of hair which enveloped a face which he liked to purse up into the image of a monkey there beat a heart as large as a football. No man was more passionately sincere in wanting to make the world a better place, no man changed his mind more often as to how it should be accomplished. What is certain is that through the Left Book Club he contributed to a change in the political climate of this country just as Allen Lane radically broadened people's outlook by making knowledge freely available at a price which they could afford.

Victor was a man of massive contradictions. As a one time fellow traveller of the extreme left – his partners in the Left Book Club were John Strachey, a communist at that time, and Harold Laski – he was the most individual of men, running his business like a dictator. As an ascetic he loved food and expensive wine with all the greed of a gourmand. As a Jew he became converted to his own individualistic brand of Christianity. If he changed his mind, which he did with the same regularity in which he changed his moods, he expected those around him to change their minds to conform with his. He was perfectly well aware of his inconsistency – the end justified the means – and when one boiled with rage he would charm you back to good humour with a self-deprecatory Jewish anecdote and a giggle of delight at the success of his story. It was impossible to be angry with Victor for long.

We stayed with him sometimes at his country house at Brimpton where his great joy was to open a bottle of champagne on the Sunday morning and drink it in the garden. And he and Ruth used to stay with us in our small cottage in Kent where my daughters still remember lying scared upstairs as Victor roared at Ruth over the bridge table (he indulged from time to time in manoeuvres which would certainly have excluded him from the

Portland Club). Next day he would charm them at lunch singing a favourite song about Rhoda, who had cider inside her, and which ultimately fermented and 'Rhoda blowed away'. 'Please make a face like a monkey, Mr Gollancz,' they would demand. And Victor would gladly comply. He was later to include their names in the dedication to *A New Year of Grace*, as Dorothy was also to feature in *Reminiscences of Affection*.

I like to think of Victor in his carefully contrived slum of an office. The floor was always littered with screwed-up balls of paper which the cleaners were forbidden to touch. The walls were covered with graffiti of which the main feature consisted of drawings of Colonel Moses, VC. Moses was Victor's alter ego. In appearance he resembled a human form of pterodactyl. He wore a top hat and travelled on a peculiar scooter. Victor and I passed many pleasantries in which Moses participated and here I quote a typical letter. I have long since forgotten the cause of the interchange on behalf of 'my lord Seth'. The style and content are sufficient.

My Lord Graham,
You will perhaps find it in your great heart to forgive me if I say, with unfeigned humility, that I by no means share the displeasure mentioned in your gracious letter to my Patron dated the 23rd August in the year of our Lord 1962, and in the 5737th year since the Creation of the World by the President. My Patron, who is extremely scrupulous in these matters, could not, in my humble opinion, have possibly interpreted the triad of words 'private and confidential' as implying that, in writing to the lord Seth (as, I understand, He told you He would be doing, without any demur on your part), He should suppress the fact that the information had come from you, it being obvious (at least to my admittedly inferior intelligence) that my lord Seth could not have imagined any other personal provenance.

My Lord and Patron interpreted those words as referring only to 'third parties', and as words that are invariably and rightly used by anyone giving information about anyone's disreputable conduct.

In conclusion, may I perhaps make so very bold as to quote what I said to my Patron when He did me the high honour of discussing the matter with me. I, Moses, Lieutenant-Colonel and nearly VC, said to Him, 'If my lord Watson had not wished, in writing to my lord Seth, to mention the source of His information, why did my lord Watson not say so, either in the body of his first gracious communication or when You, my Patron, during a verbal colloquy over the electric telephone with my lord Watson, mentioned that He would be taking the matter up with my lord Seth?

With apologies for my unwarrantable boldness in addressing you at all, and praying that, when I next venture in your Residence (for the purpose of cheating on behalf of my Patron and his celestial Lady Wife at bridge), you will not apply to me – as, I apologise to remind you, you have frequently done in the past – your footgear.

I remain, with my 'umble duty

It was not easy to conduct business with Victor when Colonel Moses, nearly VC, was introduced into the act.

At the time of which I write the Left Book Club had ceased to exist, overtaken by the war and a peace in which Victor's energies became increasingly engaged in helping to ameliorate the suffering in Germany, work which brought him a high honour at the hands of the German president. His list still reflected, but to a decreasing degree, his political affinities but increasingly a large section of it was of American origin, bought on his annual visit to America. Many of these American purchases were bought over a luncheon table 'on the nod' – to use his own expression – and some of his happiest days were spent responding to the challenge of these buying jaunts. He and Ruth used to stay in a small hotel with a tiny kitchen in their apartment. The day was spent in publishing offices, the evenings socializing, and the nights reading. Victor needed scarcely any sleep and Ruth trained herself to produce endless cups of tea as the manuscripts piled up on the floor. I returned with them once on the *Queen Mary* – Dorothy had not made that trip to New York. We played bridge every night. Our fourth was a shipboard encounter who was appropriately called Mrs Diamond. 'Did you say a diamond, Mrs Diamond?' asked Victor whenever he could, and Ruth and I had difficulty in keeping straight faces.

Victor's publishing plainly reflected his interests – and no one else's – but although he published many books because he thought they ought to be published, knowing they would make a loss, his list as a whole was as commercial as any in London. He was the first to standardize his jackets – and who of the period will forget the glaring yellow with magenta lettering? He was the first to revolutionize publishers' advertising by buying huge spaces each Sunday in the *Observer* and *The Sunday Times*. He was early to recognize the value of standard book sizes, bulk-buying of paper, cut-price printing and keeping production costs cut to the bone. Perhaps he was not the first to discover the value of employing principal book reviewers as outside readers for his firm. If there were losers on his list, due to his idiosyncratic taste, he saw to it that there was a Daphne du Maurier or an A. J. Cronin or a Dorothy Sayers to balance them. There was no list in London of its size more personal and at the same time more commercially successful.

Victor took his lunch daily at the Savoy and I recall two encounters there which demonstrate two aspects of his character. The first concerns Howard Samuel, a millionaire who had made his fortune by acquiring property cheaply during the war. Samuel had recently entered the book trade by buying the small firm of MacGibbon and Kee and made no secret of the fact that he intended to use his money quickly to advance his ambitions in a trade which he appeared to think could be run on the same lines as estate agency. He invited Victor to lunch with him at, as it happens, the Savoy. After the preliminaries had been disposed of, he said, 'Mr Gollancz, I just wanted to tell you I am going to

publish the next book by Michael Foot.' 'But,' said Victor, out-
raged, 'I have Michael under option and he is an old and dear
friend of mine. What makes you think he would countenance such
an impudent suggestion?' Samuel put his hand in his trouser
pocket and pulled out his loose change. 'How much of this have
you got, Mr Gollancz?' Victor rose from the table without a word
and left the restaurant.

Perhaps this is as good a place as any to write of my own
encounter with Samuel. I was lunching at Rules, round the corner
from the office, when I received a message from Randolph
Churchill who was lunching at the Savoy Grill to come as soon
as possible to meet Samuel whom I had never previously encountered. There was a half-empty brandy bottle on the table
and I suspected that both men had enjoyed a good lunch. 'Kind
Mr Samuel wants me to write a life of Anthony Eden,' said
Randolph. 'I said you would talk to him now and fix up the
terms.' I started to mumble all sorts of reservations such as the
fact that Randolph was already under option and would it not be
better if I rang Samuel in the morning at his office. It did not seem
to me a propitious moment for doing business. Samuel leant
across the table and said to me: 'You're talking like a bloody
literary agent.' 'I'd rather talk like a bloody literary agent than
a bloody estate agent,' I said. Samuel flushed. 'Because of that
remark,' he said, 'I will never do business with Curtis Brown.'
'When you've been in the book trade a little longer,' I said,
'you'll learn that it is not publishers who decide whether they'll
do business with Curtis Brown, but Curtis Brown who decide
whether they will do business with them.'

Samuel drowned shortly afterwards in a few feet of water when
bathing in the Aegean.

The other encounter at the Savoy concerns David Cornwell
who writes under the name of John le Carré. As reported to me by
James Kennaway, le Carré's friend, the relationship between
Victor and his author up to the publication of *The Spy Who Came in
from the Cold* was slightly strained. At that point le Carré had
written two books, neither of which had attracted much atten-

tion. With the huge success of *Spy*, le Carré felt he must make peace with his publisher and he decided to ask him out to lunch. Where best in London to entertain a distinguished figure? Surely the Savoy, and the appointment was duly arranged. As they advanced into the restaurant the maître d'hôtel came forward. 'Good morning, Mr Gollancz. Your usual table by the window?' In vain le Carré protested that it was his party and that he had booked a table in his own name. They made a royal progress through the restaurant to Victor's table overlooking the river, and then began the ritual presentation of the menu. 'I'll have my usual,' said Victor. And so the meal progressed. Le Carré who, at that time, was not a daily luncher at the Savoy, felt that somehow the occasion had fallen flat. Shortly after, and doubtless for quite other reasons, le Carré transferred his books to Heinemann.

I said that Allen Lane was the other great publisher of my lifetime. It would be hard to think of anyone who had so little in common with Gollancz, but Lane's contribution to the intellectual and cultural life of this country can surely be equated with the BBC's promotion of serious music. Lane was not himself a man of any great intellectual capacity, nor someone with a particular sense of mission and it could be argued that the Penguin triumph was an accident of timing. Certainly books had been published previously at a price as low as sixpence. Benn, for instance, for years had been publishing illustrated classics at a price of seven pence. Nor was there anything remarkable about a paperback. Hodder and Stoughton had for ages been bringing out books in paper covers at varying prices. Perhaps it was the Penguin format, or the choice of the first twelve titles, or the inaugural marketing through Woolworths, or the coming of the war, or an amalgam of all these factors which started the bandwagon rolling. Certainly no one would dispute Lane's brilliance in exploiting this early success. Nor, I think, would anyone dispute that his supreme gift was his ability to pick his principal staff and, having picked them, keep them. Later, and perhaps that was the moment when Penguin started to lose its unique position, his skill in making the right appointments appeared to desert him, but one can scarcely overestimate the contribution of Eunice Frost in creating their fiction list, nor the outstanding ability of W. E. Williams in the development of Pelicans.

Like many very successful men, Lane was not particularly popular with his contemporaries – the English can rarely forgive success – nor did he appear to be remotely bothered by this. He never much minded whose toes were trodden on once he had set his sights on some goal. At one time he was trying to make arrangements for publishing in America. At least three leading American publishers believed they had been granted his concession and he is still quoted in New York publishing circles as a good product of 'perfidious Albion'. There was also the Bumpus affair which, at the time, caused some amusement amongst those who were not directly involved.

Bumpus was a large and prominent bookshop of high quality in Oxford Street which had fallen on evil days, mainly, I believe, because of the huge rent they had to pay for their premises. A consortium of publishers, largely organized by Robert Lusty, got together to keep the shop going on a cooperative basis. Lane was an active supporter of the scheme which he enthusiastically endorsed. The principal problem was to find the right man to run it and the unanimous choice fell on Tony Godwin who was then making a substantial mark at Better Books, in Charing Cross Road. Tony, however, was scarcely installed in Bumpus before Lane offered him a much better paid job as senior editor with Penguin. Those who were left holding the Bumpus baby were not wholly delighted and, as it transpired, Lane had acquired rather a hot potato at Harmondsworth. Tony was a brilliant, mercurial character whose publishing reputation on both sides of the Atlantic was about as considerable as the size of the un-earned advances which his books were in deficit in the accounts of the publishers who employed him. Ultimately, after an enormous buying programme which weighed Penguin down for years after his departure – although conceivably improving the image of their fiction list – he left for Weidenfeld and Nicolson having, so it was said, met Allen Lane head-on over a new style of jacket that he wanted to introduce for Penguin fiction.

Lane, towards the end of his life, was tormented by the problems of succession and continuity. Eventually he entered into an arrangement with Longmans, then run by Mark Longman, a most distinguished and honourable publisher, which appeared to be an ideally complementary arrangement for both companies. But Mark died of cancer at a comparatively early age and both firms passed under the control of the huge Pearson conglomerate who gave every appearance of surprise at their new acquisition. The ensuing *angst* was to keep the book trade amused for the next few years. But that is another story. For 'it's a long lane which has no turning'.

CHAPTER NINE

T HE commonly accepted image of men constantly in the public eye is nearly always a gross distortion of their private personality. The television persona of Malcolm Muggeridge as an apocalyptic prophet of disaster is ludicrously untrue to this gentle and understanding man. The weekly performance of Bernard Levin, slaying dragons and irritating the Establishment, bears no relation to the man of goodwill and gentle disposition who lies behind the shaving-brush hair style. And the public image of John Steinbeck was a travesty of the private individual.

Elaine and John Steinbeck entered our lives in 1952 when they were in London on their way to Rome. That meeting set the pattern for a friendship which quickly deepened. After an inaugural lunch, whilst Dorothy and Elaine went on some feminine excursion up Bond Street, John and I repaired to Hardy's – always his most important call in London. Here he bought a rather ridiculous fishing hat covered in salmon flies (the first of numerous bizarre purchases which we were to make together). A few days later I sent him a telegram to his Italian hotel. I cannot now remember the contents except that it was mildly insulting and I signed it 'Angus of Old Muckie'. By return I received an answer. It read, 'Go home, Sassenach. Signed, Black Scone.'

One of the strongest recollections I have of a friendship which continued until his death in 1969 was the sheer fun of many of the things we did together. There was the occasion when John had been asked by an American film director to smuggle a great deal of jewellery out of Ireland and deliver it to a bank in Piccadilly. We knocked on the bank door well after closing time and John announced himself to the suspicious attendant as 007½ à Ian Fleming. (For some time after he wrote to me as 007¾.) For the occasion he was wearing a striking cloak which he had bought on a previous visit. For a change he had made that purchase without my being present but he wrote to me about it afterwards.

> I walked over to Gieves in Bond Street and bought a navy boat-cape, very beautiful. It is lined with white silk and has a gold chain at the throat. They telephoned the Boat Show and found that the scarlet lined one was Royal Marine's and besides made for a woman. But I do like the one I have. I tried to get a Lion and Unicorn badge for my new cap but they are or were out of them. You remember the kind we bought and polished? I wonder if you would consider buying a couple of things there for me when you are in the neighbourhood. I would like two of those cap ornaments and also a silver or white metal throat-chain with supporting lion hooks for the boat-cape. These chain latches come separately and rings and pins to hold them to the cloth.

John loved acquiring sports clothes and no London visit would pass without his buying a new yachting cap or a pair of shooting boots or a heavy mackintosh. I was also used to sudden written requests from New York. One commission included the purchase of some bagpipes in the Anderson tartan, a print of the courtyard of the foreign office and a stuffed hedgehog. I had no difficulty in obtaining the first two items but the hedgehog presented problems. Finally I went to Harrods' zoo department and, of course, they instantly agreed to help. But it would, they told me, involve catching a live hedgehog and then stuffing it. John wouldn't hear of it. He was always ready to kill for the pot but he would not countenance indiscriminate slaughter.

He was an intensely physical man. He loved the sound of a line stripping off a reel, the feel of a newly honed knife, the smell of beeswaxed leather, the texture of a well-oiled rifle stock, the sound of a sizzling barbecued steak. He loved fishing or trawling for scallops in the creek at his beloved country retreat in Sag

Harbour, followed in the evening by lots of whisky by the sitting-room fire and a simple but delicious meal. Elaine is a marvellous cook and there was nothing primitive about the establishment other than the wooded garden leading down to the water where the boats were moored. John loved gardening and watching the vegetables push through the soil. One year he and Elaine spent the summer in a cottage in Somerset. He wrote:

> Our garden is overgrown and full of trash but with the help of a schoolboy on vacation I am getting it cleared. And I have a fine scythe (borrowed) and a sickle (owned). I shall soon have it cleared and clipped and then an area for planting will be ready. But it is still a touch sticky. I have the gardener at the Manor House as advisor – a hard-bitten, red-faced Somerset-born man who can make orchids grow on Mars. He is teaching me local gardening but what he doesn't know is that he is teaching me local speech and many things he has forgotten he knows. A mean, crusty man and one I trust. When I asked to borrow a scythe, he said cynically, 'Thee be a scythe-hand?' 'Once was,' I said. Then he watched me use the scythe in the grass and his whole attitude changed. You can't fake it if you don't know the rhythm of the scythe, any more than you can fake the clean use of an axe.

John abhorred the telephone and his friends learned to avoid it except on occasions of dire necessity. John's method of communication was a yellow foolscap writing pad covered with his neat, rather spidery, handwriting – this was also how he wrote his novels. But if his stationery was commonplace he had a fetish about his pencils which he kept at needle point, shaping them with a razor-sharp knife, with the precision of a carpenter.

As has been shown, Steinbeck liked some rather childish games and his London visits usually started with our lunching together in Soho. We would each list a chosen book in three categories: a current best-seller, a standard reference book and some relatively obscure work which one could, nevertheless, reasonably expect to be available. We then started off at the top of Charing Cross Road and called in at all the bookshops between there and Hatchards in Piccadilly. If any title was in stock, the chooser won half a crown. I never recall that more than ten shillings changed hands on any one afternoon.

The summer that was spent in Somerset had a purpose. John was re-examining the Arthurian legend which he wanted to re-tell in modern terms. The Steinbecks' cottage was in the shadow of Cadbury – traditionally the main area for the legends – but his explorations took him round England and, one weekend, we all headed north towards Alnwick which is, allegedly, 'Maiden Castle'. But first John and Elaine wanted to visit the Roman wall and we picnicked on a grey, rainy day high above Housesteads. 'I can take your winters fine,' said Elaine, too frozen and wet to eat Dorothy's chicken salad, 'but what beats me are your summers.'

We were to spend the night at my parents' country house at Rothbury, only twelve miles from Alnwick and we reached there late and tired after a long day. But John was indefatigable and, after a pause for a quick drink and supper, we were back in the car and heading across the moors.

Alnwick Castle is one of the most majestic buildings in England. It stands on a hill at the foot of which runs the river Aln crossed by a bridge on which stand two fine, cast-iron lions with tails erect. Local legend has it that they wag their tails every time a Scotsman heads north out of England. We arrived at dusk. There was still a little light in the sky. The mist was rising from the river. It was easy to conjure up visions of jousting knights and maidens in their wimples. We stood in silence looking up at the castle from the banks of the river. There were tears in John's eyes.

In 1962 Steinbeck was awarded the Nobel prize and accordingly was crucified in the press by critics who customarily ignore or try to belittle successful writers. John maintained a bluff exterior but he was hurt by the virulence of the attack. He recalled that when *The Grapes of Wrath* was originally published in 1939 there was a public uproar culminating in threats on his life. He wrote at the time to his friend and American agent, Elizabeth

Otis: 'Meanwhile the Associated Farmers keep up a steady stream of accusation that I am first a liar and second a communist.' But he was neither a liar nor a communist and the book which helped to change part of the social climate of America is still as widely read as ever.

The thought of the ceremony in Stockholm appalled him:

Elaine has me now equipped with tails and owning them. Had there been a Moss Bros. here I would not have consented . . . I am working on the speech I have to make and I hate it. It will be my first speech and, D.V., my last and this may be by acclamation. Good God, everyone asks me what I'm going to say and Elaine what she's going to wear and I'm really sweating blood trying to get something down. I could write it for F.D.R., for Kennedy or for Adlai Stevenson, but I'm having one hell of a time writing one for myself.

The Nobel presentation was followed shortly after by an official, sponsored lecture tour of the USSR. John was delighted at the student seminars which gave him an opportunity to meet some of the young Russians, but came away profoundly gloomy at practically everything else. Early in the trip he and Elaine had confirmation that their bedroom was bugged, so each night they used to make a point of addressing the bug about the day's doings and passing on any complaints they wished to make to the authorities. The method proved effective. On one occasion Elaine complained of a headache. Next morning a bottle of aspirins was beside her place at breakfast. Their private conversations took place in the bathroom against a background of running water.

When John died in 1969 Elaine gave Dorothy and me a little statue of Don Quixote:

It was given him by a Russian friend in 1962, the year of the Nobel Prize, and in some ways I think he preferred the Don! Thereafter he kept it on his desk – and took it to the country in the summer. I know he'd like it to be on your desk now.

I treasure Don Quixote but I need no such reminder to keep my love for John alive.

There was more than the similarity of Christian names between John Steinbeck and John O'Hara. Both started their writing careers at about the same time and both had early success with best-sellers published shortly before the war in which they were soon to serve as war correspondents. O'Hara had an instant success with his first book, *Appointment in Samarra*, consolidated by *Butterfield 8*, two novels published respectively in 1934 and 1935. Both, at various times, engaged in journalism and stints of screenwriting in Hollywood. Both had the reputation in their early days of drinking too much and being hell-raisers. Each had affection and respect for the other. Those were some of the similarities. But the differences were greater.

In the years I knew John O'Hara – that is to say, from the early fifties – he was far from being a hell-raiser. In fact, he was a man who, with uncomplaining courage, rose above physical disabilities which would have demoralized someone of lesser character. Cured of his alcoholism only at the price of never drinking again, he had digestive problems that prevented him from eating anything but the lightest food. I cannot remember him eating anything except an omelette accompanied by a glass of milk – a diet to depress anyone – and John, for years, had been accustomed to the best of everything. Allied to his stomach problems he had trouble with his back which kept him in permanent pain and involved his continual wearing of a steel corset.

It is not surprising that, suffering from disabilities which enforced on him the most restricted of lives, he devoted his entire energies to writing. The volume of work he produced in his last twenty years – and between 1940 and the end of the war he wrote no books – is evidence of his creative energy. His daily routine towards the end of his life went something like this. He would rise at noon and have a light lunch with the inevitable glass of milk. After lunch he and his third wife, Sister, would play Scrabble until about six o'clock when they would turn on the television for a couple of hours. At eight o'clock there would be another light meal, after which John would retire to his study and work through the night until about four o'clock when he went to bed. It was not the life of a writer enjoying enormous professional success.

Although John was making a great deal of money he thirsted after the Establishment honours and, whilst awarded several, the greatest escaped him. He was generous in his congratulations to Steinbeck when the latter was given the Nobel prize and cabled him: 'Congratulations, I can think of only one other author I'd rather see get it.' For years he believed he might receive the honour himself and talked freely of tentative approaches that had been made to him. There is no doubt that he was infatuated with the trimmings of wealth and the social acceptance that he thought went with it.

Intensely Irish in background he was, rather surprisingly, a tremendous Anglophile. His stable of cars in his house near Philadelphia included a Rolls Royce, a Rover, a Triumph and an MG. His shoes and clothes came from London. In later years he and Sister made regular visits to Claridges although, apart from theatre-going, I doubt whether he got much pleasure from such occasions. I remember one disastrous outing on which we started out with the highest hopes.

John expressed a wish to hire a motor-boat from Chelsea Reach and cruise up the Thames for a picnic. The time of year was April and I tried to persuade him that the English spring was a fickle lady. He was not to be put off, but there were no boats to be hired before Kingston and foolishly I made no prior exploration of the countryside up-river. In fact there is mile after mile of uniform suburban dwellings. After two hours' cruising we were no nearer reaching the blossoming English countryside of John's imagination. Inevitably the day was bitterly cold, shot with constant showers and the boat, although the most expensive that I could hire, was a travelling slum. Dorothy, Sister and I ate a rather uninspiring picnic from a Fortnum hamper. John chewed an egg sandwich and drank some milk. The rain poured down and we cowered in the dirty cabin peering out at suburbia. The trip could not be rated a success.

John, perhaps unexpectedly, hated publicity. He tended to be pretty rough on any intrusion by the press and, in turn, the press tended to be pretty rough on him. One year his English publishers persuaded him to go through the conventional selling hoops. He hated it. The programme culminated with a Foyles lunch in the Dorchester. John took a great deal of trouble with his speech and proceeded to read it – always a counsel of despair for the after-dinner speaker. Half-way through he dried up with nerves and the chairman had to take his pages from him and finish the reading.

John was always interested in genealogy. It was important to him that a man should be able to trace his forebears. One day I got a letter from him:

There was a James O'Hara, son of John, who was born in 1752, came to Philadelphia, became a captain in Washington's army and, eventually, was the first Quartermaster General of the Continental Army. He was a founder of Pittsburgh. I believe he originated in County Mayo. My grandfather, Michael O'Hara, was born in 1839 in a place called Ballina, County Mayo. He came to this country when he was about one year old. He was an officer in the Union Army during the Civil War. He died before I was born, so we never got very closely acquainted. Too bad. He was quite a guy, a real swashbuckler.

I would like to have your solicitor, if possible, find me a solicitor in Ballina, County Mayo. Through the Ballina man I would then proceed to investigate the connection, if any, between my branch of the O'Hara clan and that of James O'Hara of the Continental Army. The Ballina lawyer would no doubt work with a genealogist, but I prefer to make my connection with a genealogist through a recommended lawyer.

The purpose of this investigation is to establish my

eligibility for one of the American ancestor-worship societies. It is called the Society of the Cincinnati, was founded by officers of Washington's Army and the first James O'Hara probably was one of the original members of it.

Interestingly enough, another O'Hara, Charles, was a.d.c. to Lord Cornwallis. When Cornwallis surrendered to Washington at Yorktown, he sent his sword to General Charles O'Hara. It is, therefore, quite possible that I was represented on both sides at Yorktown. That's as far back as I care to go, although O'Hara is one of the eight oldest names in Ireland, going back to the 9th century. The Irish know that, as I found out when I was in Dublin a few years ago. My maternal grandfather was also of pre-Revolutionary stock, but I have all the information on him.

I am full of small plans. I am also thinking of buying a thoroughbred in Ireland and racing him here next year.

I last saw John O'Hara in America in 1968. Dorothy and I stayed the night in their house near Philadelphia. John and Sister interrupted their nightly routine to give a dinner party for us. John drank the inevitable milk and about midnight retired to his study to write. His last trip to England took place early in 1970. I was surprised and saddened to hear of his death in April of that year. And I was touched that his last novel was dedicated to me.

CHAPTER TEN

O NE of the symptoms of growing older is a tendency to under-value the present and over-value the past. This is especially easy to do at a time when standards have dramatically declined and quality given way to quantity in almost every area of life. I am very aware of all this when comparing the publishing figures of the immediate past with those of the present day but the fact remains that I have worked in the book trade for a long time and it therefore inevitably follows that many of the personalities I know or knew best are no longer active on the publishing scene. Still, it's always fun to make direct comparisons and a good place to start is with the late Jonathan Cape, founder of the firm bearing his name, and the brilliant Tom Maschler who is in charge there now and has restored the image which had begun to fade after the death of its principal. Superficially, no two men could be more different. Tom, young, iconoclastic, with the bubbling energy of the Continental and a contempt for the flaccid conventions of the English; Jonathan, self-made, tough, an old dog who knew every trick in the kennel. Do they have anything in common? Charm, taste, perception and that instinct which cannot be taught and which makes the great publisher. I so well remember the lunches with Jonathan in the Edwardian block where he had a flat furnished without taste and completely devoid of the elegance which one associated with Cape books. These were designed by his partner and helped to make the firm, at the time, one of the most fashionable in London. Jonathan would sit, smiling and gossiping while his badly-fitting false teeth clicked away as we worked through the unappetizing food.

Admitted that part of the success story of Cape was due to his partner Wren Howard (a classic conjunction of opposites), just as Tom Maschler would doubtless acknowledge the different gifts of his colleague, Graham Greene, nephew of you-know-who.

Or here is another example. One of the most distinguished firms in the last fifty years or so of American publishing is Alfred Knopf now, alas, a unit in a huge conglomerate. That it has managed to retain its individuality is largely due to its present publisher, Robert Gottlieb. Bob, in my experience, conducts most of his business prone on the floor of his office. He will be wearing a shabby pair of jeans and a jersey with a hole in each elbow. Occasionally he will rise to his feet to show you the view of the East River which can be seen from the huge and elegant block which houses the group's offices. Or he will offer you some coffee – who perpetrated the legend that American coffee is more drink-able than English? – in a thick mug which is probably inscribed with some joke or aphorism. Bob loves toys (which fill his office), gadgets and *objets trouvés*. He is much loved and certainly one of the great contemporary publishers of America.

Compare Bob to the founder of that distinguished imprint. I cannot claim friendship with Alfred Knopf but Dorothy and I once had the pleasure of travelling with him on the *Queen Elizabeth*. Alfred knew no one on board. We had met briefly on some previous occasion and a routine soon developed. All day Alfred would read the manuscripts he had acquired during his trip to Europe. Every evening, after dinner, we met for a drink in the Smoking Room and I listened to the wit and wisdom of a publisher regarded by my contemporaries as a God-like figure. I shall never forget the meal we ate in the Verandah Grill on the last night of the voyage when Alfred, a noted gourmet, decided to challenge the skill of the ship's chefs!

Blanche Knopf was also an extraordinary character. Annually, she would take over a suite in Claridges where she would hold court. There she would summon anyone she wanted to see in London. She was small, elegant, beautifully dressed, and with fingernails which were long, blackcurrant-painted talons. I believe she could scratch! It was years after my first visit that I learned she was nearly blind and could read only with extreme difficulty the manuscripts of her famous authors. Fashions change, style remains. Blanche and Alfred Knopf had style in ample measure.

Martin Secker is one of the first publishers I remember meeting. For some reason I cannot now recall his firm seemed a possible alternative to my joining Nicholson and Watson and Angus arranged the introductions. At the time Secker, who had a small, distinguished list – Norman Douglas, who wrote *South Wind* was one of his authors – had fallen on hard times and was ready to take on apprentice publishers if the payment was adequate. I visited him in his small office in the Adelphi but Angus considered the fee too high and nothing came of the encounter. Shortly after the firm was bought by Fredric Warburg who recently celebrated his eightieth birthday at a dinner in his honour attended by most of the high brass of the book trade.

Fred is a tall, handsome figure of somewhat daunting mien. He usually wears a pepper-and-salt check suit, and an old-fashioned Humphrey Bogart homburg. A cigarette in a long holder always sticks out of one side of his mouth. He used to have a reputation for being aloof. I never found him so. He, like the firm of Alfred Knopf, acquired a distinguished list of European authors but the greatest jewel in his crown was George Orwell. I doubt whether the firm in his day ever made much money and some years ago it became part of the Heinemann Group. It is now managed by Tom Rosenthal, another of the young Turks of the English book trade and one of its most brilliant publishers. It is strange how distinguished publishers are so often succeeded by distinguished publishers. Or perhaps it is not. . . .

Following the war I found that, should I so wish, I could have the use of six tons of paper per annum. This, while there was still rationing, was the allocation for anyone returning from the armed services who had been a *bona-fide* publisher before the war. At the time I was on the *Spectator* and had neither the money nor the desire to set up again in publishing. However, six tons of paper was a marketable commodity so I claimed my allocation and founded the firm of Graham Watson Limited. The next problem was to decide what to do with the paper. I sought the advice of the late Harold Raymond, then and until his retirement, the senior partner of Chatto and Windus. I made this approach on the basis of a very slight acquaintanceship, deriving from the fact that he had been a neighbour of my brother Bernard. Harold was helpful, as he would always prove to be, and soon afterwards I entered into an arrangement with his firm – which lasted throughout the remaining short period of paper rationing – whereby certain of the steady backsellers from the Chatto and Windus list would be reprinted under a joint imprint. Chatto's were short of paper, I had some and it suited us both. It also led to a friendship with other members of the firm which has lasted to this day.

Dorothy and I, before we bought our own cottage, often stayed with Harold and Vera in their charming manor house in a small Kentish village where they were converting a field into a delightful garden. Harold, whose knowledge of gardening was scant, was a man of daemonic physical energy and building was his hobby. While Vera got on with the serious gardening work of bedding and planting Harold would run up yet another Grecian temple or produce some startling new lakeland vista. Both he and Vera were culture vultures of a high order and were never happier than in the galleries and churches of Venice or Florence. It took me a long time to develop a tactic to cope with Harold's discourses on our European heritage: it was to ask him firmly what he thought, for instance, of the Tintoretto in the Convent of San Marco. He was far too polite and gentle a character to tell me there was no Tintoretto in the Convent of San Marco. He would smile sweetly and ask my opinion of it.

Another partner, who, as I write, is chairman and managing director of the firm, was Norah Smallwood. There are still comparatively few women running large publishing houses and Norah was one of the first and is certainly one of the best. We were very happy when she consented to become godmother to our daughter Sophie. Her fellow godmother was Barbara, an ex-sister-in-law.

At the post-Christening lunch Barbara, who was glamorously en-shrouded in a hugely expensive sable coat, was loudly expressing her view that Beverly Nichols was our best contemporary writer. Norah listened to this drivel with mounting irritation and could finally contain herself no longer. She leant down the table and said, 'Barbara, *I* know about books, *I'll* do the talking about authors. *You* tell *us* how you got that fur coat.'

Another of the great publishing figures of this period was Jamie Hamilton who, approaching eighty, is still active in his firm. Hamish Hamilton Limited was founded in 1931, almost the last of the great prewar imprints which are still flourishing today and which include Faber and Faber, Gollancz, Cape and Michael Joseph. Hamish Hamilton developed out of the London office of Harper and Brothers, the American firm which is now called Harper and Row, which Jamie managed throughout the latter half of the twenties. It is no secret that the close association con-tinued well beyond the war years, doubtless to the benefit of both imprints.

Jamie was a great athlete; an oar at Cambridge, he rowed for an Olympic Eight, and his tennis was reputed to be on the highest amateur level. Encyclopaedic in his knowledge of the theatre and of music, he was a governor of the Old Vic before it became the National Theatre. Jamie seems to know everybody and in the book trade it is understandable that he is regarded as a rather Olympian figure moving in rarefied circles some distance from us *hoi polloi*. One can but cherish the invitation to dinner at his ele-gant house which read, 'We're not dressing, just a black tie.'

All American publishing is not centred in one place. Several well-known houses are based in Boston, at the same time main-taining a foot-hold in the main-stream with an office in New York. After three or four weeks of New York high life it was always a relaxation to spend a few days in Boston. The scale is smaller, the buildings more reminiscent of London, the park on Beacon Hill a more integral part of one's days activities than Central Park. One breathes more easily in Massachusetts.

My principal reason for going to Boston was to visit the firm of

Houghton Mifflin. An old foundation, large and much respected, it maintains an office in the London style, that is to say old-fashioned, unglamorous and untidy. I always liked their lift (I much prefer the American word 'elevator' which gives one a sense of heavenly ascent) which had an open lattice door, through which one could peer out as it ground slowly and noisily to its destination. Compared to the enclosed, high-speed elevators of New York, which leave your stomach on the ground floor, it epitomized the difference in pace between the two cities.

Two men, who became our close friends, presided over the general side of the Houghton Mifflin list – Lovell Thompson and Paul Brooks. Lovell has the bushiest eyebrows I have ever seen and obviously tends them assiduously to keep them in condition. My children used to stare at them with wonder. Lovell and his wife Kay frequently stayed at our cottage on their London visits. 'When is the man with the bushy eyebrows coming to stay?' We would be quizzed by our daughters when they were young if the gap between visits seemed longer than usual. Why they ever came, heaven knows. I used to get Lovell up into the topmost branches of an apple tree where with every appearance of enjoyment he pruned away, swaying dangerously in the Kentish gales. In London he and Kay held nightly drink parties in their flat where we would meet an improbable assortment of Houghton Mifflin authors, English publishers and the occasional agent. Kay would curl up like a cat on the hearth rug and dispense biscuits and cheese, the buttering of which occupied her attention as she listened to the conversation. She was an amateur historian and very knowledgeable about nineteenth-century American history. At one time she was writing about the Adams family. It so happened that our cottage bordered the Surrenden estate which Quincey Adams had frequently visited. Kay could not contain her excitement. Perhaps it explained why Lovell was prepared to submit to the recurring peril of the apple tree.

Paul and Susie Brooks also stayed regularly at the cottage but all such visits had to be combined with some trip where they could be certain of enduring maximum physical discomfort. Paul and Susie are really only happy when they are soaked to the skin. If they can be cold at the same time that is a bonus. They have travelled the world in search of discomfort, from Africa to Alaska, from India to Brazil. England, unhappily, could only offer them bad weather. I remember them on one holiday bicycling in the West country where they selected the parts where they would encounter the worst hills. On another occasion they took a canoe on the canals. I believe it rained every day and, soaked to the skin, they would happily bed down at night in sleeping bags under the shelter of a bridge. On this trip they were once serenaded by incredulous small boys. 'Cor, Injuns', they shouted at them derisively, as they paddled down the dark water.

No brief account of American publishing friends could omit Mike and Connie Bessie, now no longer a pair, who descended regularly on London where they were widely considered to make up a very lovable vaudeville team. Unlike most vaudeville teams, where one member acts as a feed to the partner who handles the gags, Mike and Connie gave measure for measure. Mike, now one of the most distinguished publishers in New York, has a mind like quicksilver which, combined with a sharply honed wit, makes him one of the funniest conversationalists I have ever known. Connie was never prepared to play second fiddle in this combination and any hostess was safe in handing over her dinner table for the ensuing fireworks.

Let me recount one more American anecdote: an incident which illustrates the spirit of hands across the ocean. It has long been customary for publishers on both sides of the Atlantic to use Christmas to advantage by distributing as gifts quantities of unsaleable books which are taking up expensive space in their warehouses. The hope, doubtless a pious one, is that the procedure may generate a little goodwill among the sundry recipients. I have, down the years, received a good deal of such *detritus* and to date have discovered no way in which it can be profitably disposed of.

One year Bob Lusty, as was his wont, sent the Hutchinson goodwill offering to, amongst many others, Ken McCormick, an editor at Doubleday's, with whom he had a cordial relationship. In March, three months later, he received this letter: 'Dear Bob, I am very grateful for your submission of that handsome volume *Lesser Fauna of the Creeks and Inlets of Cornwall*. We have thought about it carefully and it has received several readings but we fear it is a little too specialized for the American market. I am returning the copy under separate cover . . .'

When I look back on the riches I have received from these and other publishing friends I can see that Martin Secker was quite right to demand a fee for joining his firm. To have that much fun and get paid in addition is more than one has the right to expect.

CHAPTER ELEVEN

L ITERARY agents, as a rule, receive no training in law, yet
they must become expert in the drafting and interpretation
of contracts between publisher and author. They will be expected
to have a more than superficial knowledge of the law of copyright. They will have a working familiarity with the difference
between libel and slander. And it will be their fault only if they
are not aware of some of the more draconian implications of the
Official Secrets Act, recently the subject of a rightly abused White
Paper, which may lead, nonetheless, to reform of some of the
more objectionable provisions. I suppose these skills come to
them by a process of osmosis. Lack of them is likely to result in
bankruptcy or dismissal or, in the case of the Official Secrets Act,
a term in gaol.

If I gave a moment's thought to the Official Secrets Act during
my day to day activities it was usually to warn someone who had
served the country in an official capacity that any book they wrote
about their activities would require submission to, and clearance
from, the department concerned. It was the custom for government servants to hide their incompetence from the public by
withholding information about the way they carried out their
duties for a period of fifty years after the event. This period was
later reduced to thirty years. Thus, without the need for an
official censor, censorship was unofficially imposed. There were
those, of course, who had been in positions of great power who
ignored these regulations. Although permitted to retain their
own official papers, there were restrictions on their use. Not all
observed the rules. I believe it was Sir Winston Churchill who

first breached the regulations on a monumental scale. But the small fry had their ears cuffed and were told to behave themselves and mostly they did.

The Official Secrets Act, at least at the time of which I write, essentially consisted of two sections. The first deals with spying and any action inimical to the safety or interests of the state. It is not necessary for the State to prove that the accused's actions are a danger to the State. The onus is on the accused to prove that he is innocent. There can be few other offences under English criminal law where the accused is guilty until he proves himself innocent.

However, spies are spies and the State must protect its citizens. But Section Two is a great deal more all-embracing and it is probably true to say that it is breached several times a day by some civil servant or other – as well as politicians, journalists, broadcasters and anyone whose occupation is the dissemination of information. Essentially, the Act stipulates that any holder of an office under the Crown is committing an offence if he passes on *any* information to an unauthorized person. The section is deliberately drawn in the widest terms possible. It could, in theory, be used to protect a leak to the press about the number of cups of coffee consumed daily in Whitehall. A further subsection goes on to state that it is an offence for a person to receive any official information knowing that it is communicated in contravention of the Act. The mind boggles at the number of wives of civil servants who nightly sin as they discuss the affairs of the day with their husbands.

A further method devised to suppress news which might be embarrassing to the authorities is the issue of D-notices. This is a system, essentially voluntary – D stands for Defence – whereby the press is asked not to disclose information possibly damaging to security. The system, when responsibly administered, works well and is a useful guide to Fleet Street. Editors who refuse to conform to a D-notice can, of course, be charged with contravening the Official Secrets Act. But D-notices, irresponsibly administered, can lead to an unjustified use of censorship for the convenience of the civil servants. Frequently matters which have been freely reported abroad in newspapers on sale in this country have been by-passed by the English press for fear of prosecution.

It is probably true to say, therefore, that, since its creation in 1911, in substantially its present form, no Act has been so inimical to the interests of a free press as the Official Secrets Act. Whilst it is now generally considered that Section Two must be re-drafted in the interests of more open Government, no party in power has, to date, done more than offer lip service to such a revision.

I confess that for the greater part of my agency life I was not greatly concerned about these matters. Newspapers always seemed to me to be remarkably adept at looking after their own interests. The possibility that the editor of the *Daily Express* might one day find himself in gaol failed to keep me awake at night. So far as I was concerned, the Official Secrets Act was less a factor in my life than were regulations about parking.

I was to be rudely awakened. Early in 1970, to be precise on the morning of Thursday, January 8, I was rung up by Jonathan Aitken who reported that there had come into his possession a document bearing on the conduct of the civil war then raging between the forces of the Nigerian government and the breakaway state of Biafra. Passions as to the conduct of the war were then running very high and Jonathan thought the report might be of interest to the press. I knew that Jonathan, having recently returned from reporting the war for the *Evening Standard,* was an avid supporter of the Biafrans. I also knew that there was an active lobby in the House of Commons supporting the same cause, led by Hugh Fraser, whom I further knew to be a close friend of his. Jonathan and I discussed the contents of the document briefly on the telephone and as I gathered it was primarily a paper evaluating the military progress of the war and in parts at least highly critical of the performance of the official forces of Nigeria, I agreed that it should first be submitted to the *Sunday Telegraph,* supporters of the Biafran cause and the publisher, on previous occasions, of articles by Jonathan.

'Don't mention my name until you have their acceptance,' said Jonathan. 'After that I don't mind your referring them to me so that they can check its source.'

On returning from lunch I found the document, which was later to become notorious as The Scott Report, waiting on my desk. It was, indeed, an evaluation of the military situation in Nigeria of, to my unpolitical mind, breath-taking dullness. It was obvious that it emanated from some official source. It was marked Confidential but it had no secrecy classification nor any distribution list such as I had become familiar with at one period of my army service. As it dealt with a distant war in Africa I knew it could obviously have no bearing on the security of this country and therefore the main problem from my point of view was whether I could find any newspaper ready to publish something of so specialized a nature. However, because I could see that it was to some degree at least a classified document, I decided to ring up Hugh Fraser and seek his opinion. Although I knew Hugh to be committed to the Biafran cause I also knew that he was a privy councillor and had been Minister of Defence for the RAF in a previous government. I was prepared to follow his advice about the wisdom of submitting the report to Fleet Street.

I was fortunate to reach Hugh at the House since time was short if the article was to be published that week. He gave me all the reassurance I needed. Yes, he had indeed seen the report. Yes, he intended to raise the matter in the House. Yes, he was going to display a copy of the report in the Library of the House. Certainly it would be an excellent thing if I could find a newspaper to publish it.

Reassured, I sent it straight off to Ralph Thackeray, features editor of the *Sunday Telegraph*. I told him that I was not then prepared to reveal the source but that I would do so the moment they decided to purchase it. I mentioned a price of £750 although at that point the question of the fee had not been discussed between myself and Jonathan.

That Sunday the report was splashed across the front page of the *Sunday Telegraph*. On the same Sunday the civil war in

Nigeria came to an end with the Government forces victorious. Few newspaper scoops can have so catastrophically blown up in the face of the newspaper promoting them.

In the light of the events which were to follow, it is necessary briefly to indicate the contents of the report. Colonel Scott, Defence Adviser to the British High Commission in Lagos, produced his report 'To examine whether either side in the Nigerian Civil War can reach a successful conclusion before the end of the present dry season,' i.e., that spring. His conclusion was that the Biafrans would be overwhelmed by April 1970. So far so good – or so bad. But amongst a mass of military evaluations the report went into some detail in describing British arms supplies to the government forces of Nigeria which had, during the course of the war, grown by roughly twelvefold from their peacetime establishment. It was revealed in the report that the bulk of the arms to supply this force had been obtained from Britain. This revelation was in direct contrast to the repeated statements which had been made by the Foreign Secretary, Mr Michael Stewart, in the House of Commons. In one of them he had maintained, 'The arms which we have supplied have been broadly both in quality and quantity what we were supplying before the war began.' This was forcefully contradicted by the facts contained in the report.

The Scott Report obviously provided excellent ammunition for supporters of the Biafran cause with which to create a great political storm. The fact that the conclusion of the war coincided with the *Sunday Telegraph* publication suggested that events had overtaken what might otherwise have been a politically explosive situation. Certainly, so far as I was concerned, the incident which had made no great impression on the normal activities of a normal week was quickly forgotten.

It was, therefore, with some surprise that on the evening of Tuesday, January 27, when I was considering packing up for the day, I was informed by the girl at our reception desk that there was a Detective Chief Superintendent Pendered of the Special Branch asking to see me, accompanied by a Detective Sergeant

Digby. Naturally I agreed to see them and the reason for their visit quickly became apparent. They had just left, they said, the offices of the *Daily Telegraph* where Mr Brian Roberts, the editor of the Sunday paper, had made the statement that he had received the Scott Report from 'a literary agency of the highest repute, one with whom we deal in this field'. He had then named Curtis Brown. I was asked to confirm that I had been the individual concerned in this transaction and I naturally had no alternative but to say that I was.

I was then put under some pressure by Detective Chief Superintendent Pendered to reveal the circumstances under which I had received the report and its source. This I refused to disclose. I did not then know whether an agent's relationship with his client carried the same privileges as that between client and solicitor, but I was certainly not prepared to reveal the confidential business of my authors, unless compelled to do so. However, after further questioning, during which I became increasingly conscious that the office was now deserted and the chance of my being able to get hold of my solicitor rapidly diminishing, I was asked by Detective Chief Superintendent Pendered whether Jonathan Aitken was a client of mine. As his name was included in a readily available publicity brochure put out by Curtis Brown it seemed silly to deny the fact. It was obvious by then that the chief superintendent knew a number of facts he was not prepared to reveal to me.

By this time it was six-thirty p.m., and I asked permission to make a private telephone call. I rang Hugh Fraser and informed him of the presence in my office of the Special Branch and he gave me his authority to disclose his involvement to the two officers. They took a formal statement from me and departed leaving me in a state of some alarm.

I was to discover in the next few days that the enquiry was actively continuing. Nothing had, up till then, been discussed between Jonathan Aitken and myself concerning the *Sunday Telegraph* fee but I now received instructions from him to hold the money. It had been decided to forward the whole fee to a charity sympathetic to the Biafrans. I gave instructions for the same to be done with our commission.

And so the matter seemed to rest, although I was under no illusions that the enquiry had been dropped. By now I was deeply concerned about the possible legal implications of my own situation in the likely event of a prosecution. My solicitors were of scant comfort confirming that under Section 2 of the Official Secrets Act I had committed an offence by receiving and communicating official information 'knowing it to contravene the Act'.

On March 3 I received a further visit from Detective Chief Superintendent Pendered and his companion, Detective Sergeant Digby. I made a note of the visit:

Further visit from Pendered and Digby. They stated that they had now completed their enquiries and were shortly forwarding their report to the DPP. They stated that they had established the fact that my client was Jonathan Aitken and asked me to confirm that this was so. I said, 'As you appear to know already I see no point in denying the fact. I have throughout told you the entire truth and merely concealed the fact for the benefit of my client.' They asked what had happened to the money. I confirmed that we were holding it pending instructions for its disposal. They asked whether the asking price was in excess of the £500 received. I said it was possible but that I could not remember the exact details of the transaction and that sometimes one asked in excess of the expected figure. They asked me to identify a photocopy of the roneoed report which they had received from the *Sunday Telegraph*.

In an off the record talk they said it was their business to discover the facts and not decide on a prosecution. They said that if there was a prosecution it would be for political reasons and that as I was unpolitical it was unfortunate that I had been involved in the affair. They said that even if I was not prosecuted I could easily be a witness. They said,

'This is a messy affair and if you had known what was behind it you would not have touched it with a barge-pole.' To this I agreed.

By this time I was extremely rattled. The prospect of a prosecution was enough to keep me awake at night. Even the thought of appearing as a witness in a trial at the Old Bailey was unnerving. The time had come to look to my legal defences and I therefore acquired one of the best lawyers in London and privately consulted one of the leading prosecuting counsels at the Bar. To the former I wrote:

Dear . . .

Not only will this be a political trial, it will affect Fleet Street in a sensitive area. Although I haven't been charged it would seem to me probable that I may have innocently committed a technical offence. In any event I have no wish to advance an opinion in Court which could be damaging to the defence. Clearly I will tell the precise truth so far as I am able but there are certain actions which may require an explanation and I would like to know how much latitude I will be allowed.

I am mainly bothered by four possible questions that may be put to me:

1   Did you know the document was secret?

2   Did you query Jonathan Aitken as to its source?

3   Why did you ring Hugh Fraser?

4   Why did you agree to forgo your commission?

These would be my answers:

1   Yes, I knew the document was secret in the sense that it was not written for general publication. It did not strike me that I breached the Secrets Act because my first reaction was that this was a civil war in a foreign country, and the security of this country could not be affected. Moreover I knew the *Sunday Telegraph* had an experienced law department far better equipped than I to consider such matters.

2   No, I am used to journalists not wishing to reveal their

sources. I had assumed it came into his hands through the Biafran lobby.

3   Because I wanted to check on its authenticity and I had been told that he had a copy on which questions were being asked in the House. As he's an ex-Minister and Privy Counsellor I wanted to know whether he approved of the proposed handling of an obviously political issue.

4   Because it is the policy of this firm to associate their earnings in all matters with whatever sums are returned to their clients.

Points on which I would like your guidance:

1   Would I be permitted to embroider the explanation of why I was furthering the publication of a 'secret document'? e.g., possible public interest, *all* Government documents have some sort of classification, no inclusion of the normal classification which usually appears on military documents.

2   I have not revealed to the police that subsequent to publication I learned how he had obtained it.

3   I have not revealed to the police that the decision about the money was made after the police enquiries began.

I wonder whether we could have a meeting together as I would much value your advice.

Whilst these matters were being decided I received a summons to appear, but only as a witness, at the City of London's Guildhall Magistrates Court on April 22.

The hearing of the evidence extended over two days with an uncomfortable ten days' adjournment between and, I think, to no one's great surprise, the defendants were committed for trial at the Central Criminal Court at the Old Bailey.

This is a personal account of my only involvement, to date, with the forces of law and order and I do not intend to go into the extremely complicated issues which came up during this trial. Anyone who is interested will find it fully reported in the daily press of the period because the case attracted a great deal of attention. Anything to do with the Official Secrets Act is of compelling interest to Fleet Street and the present case involved as defendants a newspaper editor, an experienced journalist and a distinguished army officer. The latter had unwittingly been the channel by which The Scott Report had found its way to the main prosecution witness, a General Alexander, from whom Aitken had obtained it under circumstances in some subsequent dispute. Jonathan Aitken also later wrote a book on the case and the implication of the Official Secrets Act called *Officially Secret*, which should be read by any one interested in the subject.

For myself, I viewed my attendance as a witness at the Old Bailey with only a small degree of satisfaction that I was appearing as a witness and not, as might easily have been the case, as a defendant. I confess that I was somewhat overawed by the panoply of the court. I was aware that any statement of mine could affect the fate of the defendants who sat isolated in the dock. The well of the court seemed to be filled by barristers, their juniors and the supporting solicitors. The Judge, Mr Justice Caulfield, looked magisterial in his red robes – he seemed to me quite capable of donning a black cap if he chose to think I was in error. There is no doubt that, innocent or guilty, the full panoply of justice is fearful to behold.

I gave evidence for some two hours. The heart of it was reported the following day in *The Times:*

Mr Jeremy Hutchinson, QC, for the defence of the *Sunday Telegraph* and Mr Roberts: Was anything said by Mr Fraser which caused you to think that you might be committing an offence against the Official Secrets Act if you offered the report to the *Sunday Telegraph*?
Mr Watson: No, rather the contrary.
Mr Hutchinson: You appreciate that the suggestion being made in this court is that the *Sunday Telegraph* knew or had reasonable grounds for believing when they received the Report that it was being communicated to them in contravention of the Official Secrets Act? You had instituted your enquiries before you got in touch with that newspaper?

Mr Watson: Yes.

Mr Justice Caulfield: When you offered the Scott Report to the *Sunday Telegraph* you felt that you were doing nothing wrong?

Mr Watson: That is so.

Mr John Mathew for the Crown: Did you have the Official Secrets Act in mind when you made your enquiries before contacting the *Sunday Telegraph*?

Mr Watson: Yes, that is why I got in touch with Mr Fraser. It was a point on which I wanted reassurance.

Mr Mathew: You made no other enquiries, none from the Foreign and Commonwealth Office?

Mr Watson: No, most newspapers have their own legal department and they would make such enquiries automatically.

It goes without saying that my evidence was only one small factor in a case which dragged on for seventeen days and which ended in the acquittal of the defendants. Nor, I think, is there any doubt that Mr Justice Caulfield in his summing-up effectively insured that the implications of the Official Secrets Act needed to be rethought:

> It may well be that prosecutions under this Act can serve as a convenient and reasonable substitute for a political trial, with the added advantage of achieving the same and without incurring the implied odium ... We all recognize, do we not, that the opinion-forming and informing media like the Press must not be muzzled ... This case, if it does nothing more, may well alert those who govern us at least to consider, if they have the time, whether or not Section 2 of this Act has reached retirement age and should be pensioned off.

I look back on my involvement in the affair of The Scott Report with mixed emotions. There were the weeks of worry which followed the initial visit to my office of Detective Chief Superintendent Pendered which, to me, seemed horribly reminiscent of the dreaded midnight knock common in police States. There was the feeling of helplessness that, in all innocence, I was caught up in a situation over which I had little control. There was the final respect for the working of the law, slow and ponderous though it was, in coming to its proper decision. But it was an experience which I would happily have forgone.

CHAPTER TWELVE

I FIRST met Wilfred Thesiger through Gavin Maxwell. Gavin who had recently received some attention for his book about shark-fishing, *Harpoon at a Venture,* was living in a flat near Olympia. One noticed a musky, animal smell on opening the door and the sitting room was dominated by a wire contraption restraining an otter. I treated the animal with respect as soon as I noticed that Gavin wore steel-reinforced gloves with which to handle it. It was, I think, his first association at close quarters with one of the breed which was subsequently to make his fortune.

Gavin was a somewhat demanding author. He needed money in substantial amounts and he didn't much mind from whence it came. His new publisher, Mark Longman, to whom I had introduced him, was thought to be a useful source of supply. The telephone would ring in my office. 'Gavin here. I'm in a garage near Inverness. My supercharger has blown. It's going to cost £150 to repair. I need the cash before my cheque bounces. See if Mark will provide. I'm coming down by sleeper and we'll meet for lunch tomorrow.' I would duly report at the luncheon rendezvous to find the impoverished Gavin driving up in a Daimler, temporarily hired to replace his damaged Alvis.

Life with Gavin was life on a roller-coaster and finally we parted company when I found one of his demands went further than I was prepared to venture. But, by then, he had introduced me to Wilfred Thesiger, or rather suggested that it might be worth my while to get in touch. Gavin had recently returned from spending some weeks with Thesiger in the marshes between the Tigris and Euphrates, which subsequently became the subject of his book, *A Reed Shaken by the Wind*, and from whence he received, from Wilfred, the gift of the otter Edel which was later the subject of the world best-seller, *Ring of Bright Water*.

'Wilfred has some marvellous photographs,' said Gavin. 'They would make a lovely book.'

This was in the period before the coffee-table book became, for a short period, fashionable and therefore profitable, and the thought of a book of photographs did not set my juices flowing. However, I wrote to Thesiger and asked him for an appointment. I received a polite message suggesting that I report one afternoon to a block of flats not far from Chelsea Hospital. I was received by a tall, powerfully built man with the physique of a boxer. He had a deeply lined, craggy face featuring a nose which had obviously once been broken and which was set between piercing, grey eyes. It was a face once seen never forgotten. I quite soon grew to know it and like it.

'You've come to see some photographs,' said Wilfred. 'I can't think why. But there are plenty of them.'

He took me into his small bedroom, opened the door of a cupboard and indiscriminately threw out on to the bed half a dozen albums selected at random from a shelf containing about sixty. He stood behind me watching, but didn't speak as I turned the pages. I, in turn, found it difficult to express my mounting excitement. The quality of the pictures was superb. After a minute or two, I began asking questions. Wilfred answered perfunctorily. He was plainly bored by the intrusion and felt my interest due to superficial politeness, but I persisted and I could judge by the fact that the monosyllabic replies were lengthening into short sentences that he was beginning to realize that my wish for background information was neither formal nor polite. I stayed enthralled for about three hours at which point I felt we had established a degree of communication.

'Photographs by themselves are very difficult to sell,' I said. 'Could you not provide some accompanying text?'

'I can't write,' said Wilfred. 'I don't want to write and if I did write no one would be remotely interested.'

'At least let me see if I can find a publisher who would be interested,' I said. 'May I bring one along?'

'It would be a waste of your time and his,' he said, 'but do whatever you like.'

So next day I returned with Mark Longman and the same performance was repeated, disinterest and boredom slowly giving way to slight signs of warmth. By the time Mark and I left three hours later, Wilfred had promised, hedged by every conceivable qualification, to try his hand at writing a book. He seemed genuinely appalled at the prospect.

The following day I returned yet again, this time with Elliott Macrae of Dutton and an American publisher thus also became committed to the project. All that now remained was for Wilfred to produce his book. He decided to do this in solitary confinement, living in a hotel in Copenhagen whence, twice a week, I would receive a chapter in his meticulous, tiny handwriting. The early ones were not very good. Wilfred was simply unable to grasp that the intensity of his feeling transformed the most ordinary happenings into matters of compelling interest to the reader – he was inclined to leave these things out as being of no possible interest to anyone but himself. The last of the great lone travellers, following in the footsteps of the giant Victorian explorers, Thesiger had deliberately sought a life in the dangerous deserts, mountains and marshland of the Middle East and Africa. He detested the values of the shoddy twentieth century and had spent his life escaping from them. Emotionally, therefore, he found it difficult to accept that those who lived in a civilization he despised could, at the same time, be interested in the solitary travelling in which his life had largely been spent. My job was to try to make him loosen up and get to the core of the matter without running the considerable risk that any criticism or discouragement might wither the delicate seed of authorship before it had taken hold. Somehow our relationship prospered and with it, very quickly, Wilfred understood what was needed. He responded beyond my wildest expectations. *Arabian Sands*, written in superb, spare prose, was soon to be acclaimed as a masterpiece to equal Doughty's *Arabia Deserta*. It was followed a few years later by the equally distinguished *Marsh Arabs*. The two books have now become classics.

I feel I have been lucky in helping to bring to birth a number of books which might, perhaps, never have been written without my intervention. There are none where I have been prouder to have been the midwife than Wilfred's two masterpieces.

It has always surprised me how authors, whose principal stock in trade is an inventive gift, are so often unable to find appropriate subjects. Naturally this seldom applies to the novelist dependent on experience allied to a creative imagination, but it certainly frequently applies to the biographer, historian and non-fiction writer. Quite one of the most useful functions of the agent or publisher is to marry the right subject to the right author. Many authors are deterred because of other books already written on a subject. As a general rule I think it can be said that almost any reasonably attractive or important subject can be newly tackled every ten years or so. It does not necessarily depend on new source material becoming available. Each generation will approach a subject from a slightly different angle.

After Elizabeth Longford had received some acclaim for her book *The Jameson Raid*, she was in doubt about its successor. I suggested she write a biography of Queen Victoria, a subject much written about. I felt that Elizabeth's persistence in research, grace of style and access to the source material would create new interest in a contentious ruler. And so it proved. After the book had been published with worldwide success, Elizabeth once more asked me to propose a subject. I suggested that perhaps she should consider tackling Mary, Queen of Scots, putting the emphasis on the woman rather than the queen. Elizabeth seemed delighted at the idea and agreed to do the book but before the contract was exchanged she met the Duke of Wellington who offered to make available to her the family papers of his ancestor, the general and statesman. She was naturally thrilled to be offered such fascinating material and abandoned Mary on which she had done virtually no work. In due course her labours produced two magnificent books, *Wellington: the Years of the Sword*, and *Wellington: Pillar of State*. Mary, Queen of Scots, was forgotten.

But not quite. Shortly after Elizabeth had decided to take on Wellington I received a call from Antonia Fraser, her daughter, whom I had not met.

'I know,' said Antonia, 'that you suggested Mary, Queen of Scots, as a subject for my mother. Ever since I was at Oxford I have been intrigued by Mary and I particularly like the proposal that she be treated as a woman rather than a queen. Do you think I could possibly take it over?'

And so Mary remained in the family and, four years later, another best-seller was born.

But being an agent isn't only about best-sellers, comforting though it is when you have a few under your belt. Being an agent is about authors and they come in all shapes and sizes – as, of course, do agents. C. P. Snow once said, 'I happen to think you are a good agent, but I like you because you have never hit me, like a previous agent, and never insulted me at my own dinner table as did my American agent.' I have to confess that I have never indulged in fisticuffs, being a reasonably peaceable soul, but it seems to be an integral part of the profession. Rumer Godden, who has achieved the difficult double of capturing a children's audience almost as large as that for her adult books, once told me that her husband, James, was belaboured in the arcades of the Ritz Hotel after an especially stormy dinner with an earlier agent.

Authors, in my experience, are a likeable lot. They live an essentially solitary life, have a great need for love and reassurance and are very ready to offer it in return. But this is not always the case. One could not, I suppose, call the Conservative MP, Gerald Nabarro, an author, although it was in that capacity that I went to see him. He worked in a rather grubby office in a shabby street near Westminster Abbey which seemed an odd setting for such a flamboyant character. I climbed up a flight of narrow stairs into a small, partitioned outer office. The girl sitting there announced my arrival. Loud and clear over the telephone, as well as through the thin partition, came the booming reply, 'Tell the bugger to cool his heels.' If it hadn't been for the fact that I was professionally hungry, and rather young, I would have left. But I waited.

After twenty minutes Nabarro appeared at the door of his office wearing the transparently false smile which is sported by politicians, always alert for a potential voter.

'Mr Watson,' he said, 'how very delightful of you to have spared me the time to come and see me. *Do* come in.'

We never transacted any business I'm happy to say.

There was another politician, this time Labour, Woodrow Wyatt, who picked my brains over a glass of champagne and then wrote to say he didn't need an agent. He sent me a cheque for thirty pounds in compensation, so I forwarded it on to the Tory Campaign Fund.

On the other hand there is Martha Gellhorn, a saintly character if ever there was one – though she herself doesn't believe in saints. We met her first through St Mary's, Bourne Street, a church round the corner from our house, whose practices were slightly higher than St Peter's, Rome. It was presided over by Father Langton, another saintly figure, who arranged special children's services of instruction. Our daughters were entranced, as we were, by the bells and the incense and the constantly changing panorama in front of the altar, none of which, probably, had much to do with religion. Father Langton sometimes wandered about amongst his congregation whilst the service was in progress and you would receive a dig in the back. 'Come up to the presbytery for a dram after the service,' he would say.

St Mary's was also attended by Tom Matthews, ex-editor of *Time* magazine, who lived round the corner in Chester Square and who was married to Martha, who had previously been the wife of Ernest Hemingway. Tom had been asked to evaluate the chances of starting a British edition of *Time*. He worked hard at the project for twelve months and appeared to get much encouragement from New York. After a year or so a minion arrived in London to tell him the whole thing was off. Tom cabled Henry

Luce, the proprietor. 'Why did you keep me standing on tiptoe for so long if you weren't going to kiss me?' The cable has passed into the legend of Fleet Street.

Through Tom we met Martha who was emphatically not an attender at St Mary's. Soon Father Langton was to be stricken by a debilitating form of paralysis which made him bedridden. He disappeared to the wilds of Cambridgeshire to be looked after by his sister. His most regular visitor was Martha, who made the pilgrimage with whisky and books to argue with him about the non-existence of God. She did more than most, and certainly more than his fashionable congregation, to keep him alive.

Martha loves Kew Gardens which she regards as an oasis of peace in the racket of London. She once wrote to the curator and asked if he had a job where she could help. To be working in Kew Gardens seemed to her to be bliss. She got an answer that the staff had all to be technically qualified. 'May I,' asked Martha, 'come out and help clear up the mess after the public have been at the weekends?' So they gave her a pointed stick and a little barrow and Martha tidied up the gardens she loves so much.

Then there is Bernard Fergusson, the epitome of the British military officer as imagined by the average European – tall, handsome, moustachioed, monocled and erect as a telegraph pole. We saw Bernard from time to time when we had a cottage in Kent and he was in charge of Dover Castle where he claimed that on a good day he could see the time by the clock on Calais town-hall. Bernard, whose distinguished career embraced a variety of important posts, was colonel of the Black Watch and thus in charge of the troops at the time of Suez. During the build-up, it was reported to him that on the letters being sent home by the Jocks there appeared on the backs of the envelopes the letters RUSSIA. What was this Marxist influence that appeared to be infiltrating the troops? Bernard ordered an enquiry. It turned out the mystic rune stood for, Rogering U Some Sunday In Aberdeen.

I used, humbly but tongue in cheek, to write to Bernard with the respect due to his position. He used to reply – referring to my war-time rank in the artillery – 'Dear Acting Unpaid (unless by results) Bombardier (retired and not a moment too soon.)'

A spirited composer of light verse, Bernard penned the following:

> Courage, brother, do not stumble
> If you've got five chapters done,
> Do not be so bloody humble
> Grit your teeth and carry on.
> Though the path be dark and weary
> And the end far out of sight
> Though your prose be unco' dreary
> Screw your courage up and write.
>
> Some might say 'Submit synopsis',
> That depends on what you're at:
> If the book just growed, like Topsy's,
> It might benefit by that;
> If you're working on a novel,
> Write the ruddy thing instead;
> But you'll finish in a hovel
> Begging for a crust of bread.
>
> Have the guts of your convictions
> (Not the ones before a beak),
> Both biographies and fictions
> Falter every other week.
> Agents do not like a flutter
> They prefer the finished job;
> Agents earn you bread and butter,
> And they're worth it, every bob.
>
> Finish then your creation,
> Pure and spotless may it be;
> Send it round the whole darn nation
> But for God's sake not to me.

Try an agent; and the best one
Plies his trade in London town;
13 King Street, London West one,
Watson c/o Curtis Brown.

There's verse and verse. Roy Fuller wrote to me on a postcard on learning that an American publisher had turned down his latest novel:

I never thought that by a stupid word
Or two I'd come to rival George iii.

There are other memories that come crowding in. Of Randolph Churchill at East Bergholt and the path through the wood bordered by crimson primulas to resemble a flowing stream of flowers: of his lawn bereft of dandelions, but pitted with craters, following a garden party at which a prize of five pounds was offered for the child who produced the largest number of dandelion roots – it would have cost its owner one hundred pounds to clear the lawn by more orthodox methods! Of his daughter, Arabella, sitting on his knee, while she recited endless chunks of poetry, lovingly prompted by her father whenever she forgot a word. Of deadly late nights when the spirit flagged and bed seemed so inviting and so distant. Dear Randolph, loyal but demanding of those who served him. One remembers his story of knocking up his friend Lord Beaverbrook at Stornaway House in Green Park. The door was answered by the butler. 'The Lord is by the lake,' he said. 'Doubtless walking on the water,' replied Randolph.

There is Richard Gordon (Dr Gordon Ostlere), a one-man industry supporting depressed and run-down sporting events. If there is an unfashionable cricket match between, say, Northamptonshire and Essex, out of the attendance of seven spectators, sitting miserably in the rain and peering at the pigeons who are the solitary occupants of the cricket pitch, one will be Gordon, broaching a bottle of excellent claret and chewing a smoked salmon sandwich provided by his delectable wife, Jo. He will explain later, probably truthfully, that he was working out the plot of his next book. In winter he will be found, enshrouded in a vast teddy-bear coat and a ridiculous Russian hat, cheering on the depressed members of the Blackheath rugby club. I look back on so many happy, sporting outings with Gordon. The Garrick Club bus on its way to the University Match at Twickenham, where the champagne has been broached before we have turned the corner beside Moss Bros. The sultry days of summer at Lords when Gordon has arrived with a vast hamper filled with goodies cooked by Jo, and at least a couple of bottles of something to see us through the lazy afternoon. Gordon, for years, has made a practice of stocking up his cellar just before the annual budget. He does not, therefore, offer you a bottle of, say, Château Mouton Rothschild. 'Would you like,' he will suggest, 'a glass of George Brown or would you prefer a good Harold Macmillan?' So many books have seen the light of day under these agreeable conditions. Summer days on a Sussex lake where the trout are sufficiently tame to make both of us pleased with our piscatorial skills and the resulting celebrations at the local where Gordon consumes his 'usual', a fitting backdrop to a discussion of whether Sir Lancelot is due for retirement in the next instalment of the Doctor books. Those who have the opportunity to mix business and pleasure in such surroundings are, perhaps, not best qualified to advance an opinion about the endless strikes at British Leyland.

Yes, it is one's authors which keep one an agent. Dear, demanding, lovable, impossible clients. From time to time, of course, the tempter beckoned, most often in the guise of a publisher and sometimes it took me all of an hour to consider and decline their offers. But one invitation I sometimes like to recall.

I was rung up one day by Michael Joseph. 'Let us lunch,' he said.

'My turn,' I said, meaning that Curtis Brown would foot the bill. 'Let us meet at the Savoy grill,' I suggested, as Joseph was a distinguished member of the book trade and only the best would suffice.

On the day of the lunch I got a call from him. 'Can we change our lunch to the Savoy restaurant?' said Michael. I made the necessary adjustment to the reservation and, in due course, we sat down to lunch.

'I hope,' said Michael, 'you didn't mind me changing the venue. But you are still comparatively young in this business, and I thought you wouldn't mind me telling you that people in the book world shouldn't be invited to the grill. That's only for grey-flannelled city gents. The rest of us use the restaurant.'

I shuffled restlessly on my seat. I felt I had no need of a lesson in social manners and I remembered the many lunches I had eaten with Victor Gollancz at his table in the grey-flannelled grill room.

By now Michael obviously felt that I was sufficiently softened up.

'By the way,' he said, 'Bob Lusty is leaving us to go to Hutchinson's. How about you joining us to be our literary director?'

But by then the Savoy restaurant and Michael Joseph Ltd had lost my attention. I knew beyond doubt, then and always, that literary agency is emphatically about authors and I knew I would want it no other way.

CHAPTER THIRTEEN

FROM time to time I have been invited to address various book trade clubs and societies. The trade proliferates in such organizations, most of them giving their members an excuse for a night out in which they have the opportunity to behave like elderly schoolboys. In some they address each other as Brother This or Brother That; in others they take on the demeanour of Odde Volumes; in another the speaker has to versify in the style and spirit of Omar Khayyam. One of them, a luncheon club called the Paternosters, invites a speaker to address the gathering on a subject of his choice. On one occasion I was present when the speech was made by Robert Birley, then headmaster of Eton. 'I queried the secretary,' he began, 'as to the subject he would like me to tackle. "Anything you like," I was told. Never before have I had an invitation so amiably comprehensive. For years I have wanted to talk about the Prevalence of Elephants in Classical Literature. That, therefore, will be the subject of my talk.' So for an hour, long after the bulk of his audience had returned to their desks, he addressed us on the subject of elephants. It was a brilliant and witty performance.

My own subjects were less exciting. I would be asked to speak on '*Whither Agency?*' or '*Whence Agency?*' or, sometimes, '*Why Agency?*' Of course they all added up to the same plea. 'Tell us what you think a literary agent does, and whether there is any explicable reason why he should be encouraged to do it?'

I always found these somewhat bizarre requests. Landowners or builders do not, so I suppose, approach estate agents and ask them to discuss the purpose of their profession. City tycoons seem to manage pretty well without an address from stockbrokers discoursing about their daily activities. Why are members of the book trade – not especially remarkable for their general stupidity – so unable to fathom the mystery of how and why a small number of their compatriots earn their living?

I suppose part of the answer lies in the smallness of the profession. There are only about a dozen literary agencies of any size, and perhaps another dozen or so who manage to achieve a little more than some sort of a living. And this little band tends to be dealing in rights which, whilst of importance to the professional author and the publisher who publishes him, represents only a fraction of the gross turnover of the book trade. I have heard it said that there are publishers, presumably making a living of some sort or other, who take pleasure in boasting that they have never dealt with a literary agent and wouldn't recognize one if they saw one. Certainly until Curtis Brown and some other agents started to develop an academic side, a large proportion of the academic publishers in Britain had never had recourse to dealing with agents – and academic publishing represents the major income of the book trade.

It is a common belief, advanced by firms who, for one reason or another, are ignored by agents – nearly always because of their incompetence – that the small publisher is by-passed and only the large firm gets the agent's custom. There is a grain of truth in this, but only a grain. My own firm, for instance, made contracts at the last count with one hundred and seven publishers in one year. But it is, of course, a fact that as the agent's first duty is to look after the financial interests of his clients he has to evaluate the pecuniary, marketing and other merits of those with whom he does business.

But perhaps I should start at the beginning and try to answer the question I posed earlier. What is a literary agent and what does he do? Maybe the answer is provided by the publisher William Heinemann writing in the *Athenaeum* in 1893. He wrote:

This is the age of the middleman. He is generally a parasite. He always flourishes. I have been forced to give him some little attention lately in my particular business. In it he calls himself the literary agent. May I explain his evolution?

The Origin. You become a literary agent by hiring an office, capital and special qualifications are unnecessary; but *suaviter in modo* must be your policy, combined with a fair amount of self-assertion. You begin by touting among the most popular authors of the moment, and by being always at hand and glad of a job you will soon be able to extract from them testimonials which, carefully edited, make a seductive prospectus to send out broadcast. You must collect these testimonials with zest, just as the pill-doctor or the maker of belts electro-pathic.

Heinemann was writing at the turn of the century but it would be easy in the present day to find publishers to applaud his sentiments – not from them any appreciation of the fact that they are also middlemen interpolating their services between author and reader.

Heinemann was writing about the years that saw the inception of the literary agent. Although there are those who fancifully maintain that the profession can be traced back to the aristocrats who patronized and financed the work of their favoured author or poet, in modern terms probably the first recognizable professional agent was A. P. Watt who put up his plate in 1893. He fulfilled a need. At that time authors were being fleeced by publishers who frequently bought the copyright in a book for an outright sum. Thus, Dean Farrar's *Life of Christ* made £50,000 for the publisher, £2000 for the author. This figure is not out of proportion to the eighteen pounds which Milton received for *Paradise Lost,* the copyright of which he too sold to his publisher. W. Robertson Nicoll, writing an article on agency for the *Bookman* quotes a novelist who sold his book outright for £500, whereas his publisher went on make a profit of £19,000.*

---

* Anyone interested in pursuing this subject in greater detail should read *The Author's Empty Purse* by James Hepburn, Oxford University Press, 1968, to which I am indebted for these figures and much else.

Interestingly enough, the hostility of publishers towards agents still survives, even though there is no longer any question of exploitation on quite this scale, as most publishers must realize that it is self-defeating to fleece their authors. Nevertheless, the dramatic curtailment of this profitable activity in the past is something that the publisher still seems to hold against the agent. Stanley Unwin in *The Truth about Publishing*, still the best practical handbook to the book trade, made no effort to conceal his dislike and contempt for agents. There must be some deep-seated reason for this antipathy since it is the author, not the publisher, who pays the agent. In theory the publisher can only be adversely affected by the activities of the agent in the sense that if the latter did not exist, the publisher would generally be able to buy an author's work at a price less than that established by the working of normal market forces. Few authors know the value of their work. Why should the publisher feel that in some way he is threatened by an agent's activities?

I remember an early, if not entirely remarkable, demonstration of an agent's influence when, shortly after joining Curtis Brown, I submitted a short story to the *Evening Standard* pseudonymously and sent from my home address. I received a letter of acceptance and a cheque for seven pounds. I got on to Charles Curran, then the features editor and protested. 'Look,' I said with some annoyance, 'normally you pay fourteen pounds for a short story.' 'If you'd sent it to me from Curtis Brown you'd have got fourteen pounds,' said Charles with equal irritation, enclosing a further cheque. At about the same time – in the late forties – there was the more impressive evidence provided by the case of Dr Edith Bone.

Dr Bone was an English communist of Hungarian extraction who, for some years, had been incarcerated in Budapest in solitary confinement. Momentarily there was a pause in the cold war and Dr Bone was released from prison and returned to England. Whilst still in Hungary she had been approached by the local correspondent of the *News Chronicle* who offered her two hundred pounds to write four articles about her experiences. Dr Bone, an old journalist herself, knew that if someone volunteered to pay her £200 they were certainly worth quite a bit more. So when she arrived in London, still in the clothes she wore in prison and straight from the airport, she came along to see me, having been advised to do so by someone in the British Embassy.

'I think these articles are worth one hundred pounds each. What do you think you can do for me?' she asked.

I said I would see and I asked her what her immediate plans were.

'Get some clothes,' she said. 'I've only got this Burberry which I was allowed to keep in prison and which I used as a cushion when it wasn't being used as a blanket. Without it I would have been dead.'

I picked up the phone and rang the manager at Burberry's and told him the bones – pun intended – of her story.

'Send her round to me straight away,' he said. 'We'll be only too honoured to kit her out free.'

Whilst this was in progress I started ringing round Fleet Street. Finally, satisfied with the result, I rang Dr Bone at Burberry's.

'I've got you £5000 from the *Daily Express*,' I told her.

There was a silence at the end of the phone, then the sound of a falling body. Dr Bone had fainted.

Of course an agent's work is rarely as dramatic as this, for most of the time he is handling the work of writers who have an already established worth, or he is initiating things for the new author.

But in my thirty years or so as an agent, the balance of activity has changed as dramatically for him as it has for the publisher. Whereas both spend as much of their time as ever on seeking out and supporting the new authors who are the seedlings from which tomorrow's forest will grow, more and more of their time is being devoted to the work of the professional writer – to use a some-what misleading expression. Less than ever can an agent indiscriminately afford to act for an author solely because he produces a publishable manuscript.

How does one define the 'professional' writer, since anyone who has a book published will receive a monetary reward of some sort? Obviously the term embraces more than those authors for whom writing is their only occupation, their principal source of income. It will also include the wide range of writers whose main activities lie elsewhere but who have an attitude of mind, an innate skill, a knowledge of the market at which their work is aimed. It would exclude the very large number of writers competent enough to get their books published but whose writing is a relaxation, a hobby, a means of making a modest contribution to their income. If this is an elitist view of writing it is meant to be. Half of the troubles from which the book trade suffers derive from the number of amateurs who overburden the machine.

So, less and less does the agent represent the novelist with a sale limited to British publication, or the minor autobiography of a retired junior politician or diplomat or literary agent. Such books are still being published, to a lesser extent than previously, but they are being published as a rule without an agent being involved.

Broadly speaking, except where an author's advance is substantially unearned, publisher and author each make approximately the same amount from a book. Of course, in this calculation the publisher has covered the expenses of running his firm, whereas the author has not contributed to any of his overheads or living expenses. It is also true that many authors are financed by other sources of income than their writing. The agent is in a different situation. His earning is, broadly, ten per cent of the publisher's or author's. Thus, if a publisher has a success and makes a profit of £1000, having already covered his basic overheads, an agent's return is one hundred pounds from which he has still to recoup his overheads. Publishers expect to pay for the losses of their unsuccessful books by the substantial profits on their successful ones. This also applies to the agent, but to a lesser degree. Both make most of their money from a very small proportion of their authors.

A publisher's capital investment and his financial risk are

vastly greater than an agent's, but so are his chances of recoupment.

I have tried at times to work out what is the prime cost of servicing any individual transaction. In theory all income, however small, should be welcome as contributing to the expense of running an office. In practice, however, it is perfectly possible for a deal to cost more than it makes. An agent may for instance sell serial rights in Greece and receive fifty pounds for the transaction, which is five pounds in terms of commission. The author is delighted at his additional income and the widening of his market. The deal has probably cost the agent about fifty pounds in postage, telephone calls and accountancy. He views this outlay philosophically. Not only has he satisfied his client but he gets well-remunerated from sales made in more profitable markets. From this it can be understood why there is a widening category of authors whom the agent can no longer afford to represent. It is now a great deal easier for some writers to find a publisher than an agent.

It is, also, true that there is a wide range of writing where the writer has absolutely no need of an agent and would be better off without one. There are several reasons for an author employing an agent, but the main one is that the agent, having covered the cost of his commission, will increase his client's earnings. With the writer whose books sell a thousand or so copies in the English edition, with no likelihood of finding a market elsewhere, this is difficult to achieve. Such a writer would be well-advised to save his commission and deal direct with a reputable publisher. But what of the author already at the top of the tree, where a book by book increase in earnings is not attainable, because he has reached his maximum audience. Why do such authors retain the services of an agent? Firstly, because an agent's commission is chargeable against tax, so that the net cost of the services he provides for a writer with a substantial income is modest. More relevant, however, is the fact that by this time in the professional writer's career the agent's function has begun to change. His client's activities are by now established in a variety of fields and he now requires someone who can manage the wide range of his business and monetary affairs so that he can get on with the job of writing. If there are unexpected markets to explore they will, of course, be explored. But the author, primarily, is employing a specialist business manager at a relatively modest outlay. Such specialization on the part of the agent will, nowadays, embrace a generalized knowledge of tax law, the formation of trusts, the provision for dependants and other matters which involve the saving of tax. These are some of the reasons why the full-time writer most often uses an agent and why the agent increasingly directs his attention to the needs of the professional author.

Why cannot these functions of the agent be equally well carried out by the publisher who, in any case, does act in this capacity for the author where no agent is employed? Every publisher has a subsidiary rights department which ranges from a large specialist section consisting of, perhaps, half a dozen people to a part-time girl who does what she can after her other, more demanding, duties have been completed. In some respects the large publisher, with an experienced subsidiary rights department, will achieve better results than a very small agent, because the efficacy of both depend, to a certain extent, on the number of properties available for sale, the consequent income received and the resulting cash available to underwrite further activities. It is, for example, a great deal easier to sell serial rights to a Sunday newspaper if one is doing it often and, therefore, has a knowledge of the right price and of the paper's policy. These are requirements which can only be achieved by regular contact with the features editor. The larger the number of sales an agent makes, the greater the resulting degree of specialization he can afford.

The average small agent tries to surmount this inadequacy by employing sub-agents specializing in certain markets where he has neither the time, energy or money to deal himself. It is a workable but not, in my view, a satisfactory solution. But no one with a small client list, whether agent or publisher, can be expected to know by personal experience what, for example, the sale of a serial right to a Greek newspaper is likely to produce. The

sceptical reader may query how often serial sales to Greek newspapers are made but somewhere around the world, equivalent
minority markets constantly provide worthwhile outlets for the
right book.

I posed the question why a publisher is not just as well-
equipped as the agent to represent the author in the sale of his
subsidiary rights. By subsidiary rights I mean serial, American,
translation, film, television, dramatic, everything which can
derive from ownership of copyright. The reason why an author
is, in theory at least, better off with an agent in disposing of these
important properties is that in many instances an author's and a
publisher's interest conflict. And where a conflict arises only a
saintly publisher will put his financial gain second to that of the
author. I am not denying there may be such members of the book
trade but most publishers resolve such conflicts not by reference
to the Holy Ghost but by pretending they don't exist and that
the author's interest coincides with his. In the case of an agent
this is demonstrably the case. His only reimbursement is to
receive commission on what he has earned for his author. It is not
demonstrably the case with a publisher.

Let me quote two instances where an area of potential conflict
exists.

When a serial is sold to a newspaper it is stipulated that its
publication shall, so far as possible, coincide with the publication
of the book. In most cases newspapers are perfectly happy to
adjust their plans to any such arrangement which helps to promote the sale of the book and which is in the mutual interest of
the author, the publisher and, usually, the newspaper. But
sometimes, perhaps for reasons of extreme topicality, a newspaper wants to publish extracts long before the book can be made
available in the shops. Almost certainly the author would lose the
considerable benefits which would accrue from such a sale unless
he agreed to this premature publication. It may be that to a
limited extent the sale of the book will be adversely affected by
this early serialization. Were he to be acting for the author in such
a case he would be in a dilemma. Whose interests to pursue?

Similarly many English publishers have a loose quid pro quo arrangement with two or three American counterparts with whom they maintain a very close relationship. 'You scratch my back, I'll scratch yours. You offer me your books, I'll offer you mine.' It is possible for an author to suffer from such a restrictive arrangement. The benefit to the publisher is apparent. But the author may find himself on the wrong list on the wrong terms. The author's book is being used as counter to pay for benefits which the author will not enjoy. Agents also enjoy special relationships with publishers – if they didn't they would be ineffective as agents. But they would be fools if they allowed such relationships to affect their authors' earnings. To do so they would be restricting their own.

As a publisher is essentially in business to publish, it might be wondered why he is also so anxious to take on the functions of an agent. The reason, of course, is financial. Many publishers, especially in America, freely admit that their profit derives from their share of the special rights which they control. No longer do they expect profit to arise primarily from sales of books published under their own imprint. Currently it comes from paperbacks, book clubs and any other market where their participation is just as entrepreneurial as the agent's, since such rights are usually leased to a third party. What in fact publishers resent is the agent taking away money which otherwise would be theirs. Unable to make a profitable living from their chosen profession of publishing they try to bolster up their earnings by dealing in the market place with rights which the author and only coincidentally the publisher, has created.

A further cause of irritation is that they believe that the agent has now acquired too much power. There is a modicum of truth in this. I have no means of measuring what percentage of book trade income derives from agented books – much less than might be imagined, since the greater proportion still arises from educational, specialized and technical books, most of which are un-agented. But it is certainly true that the professional author who tends to produce the big seller which enables the general publisher to survive, does – as a rule – employ an agent. The power that this enables an agent to wield is certainly considerable and, as I explained earlier, because an agent's job is, amongst other things, to maximize his author's earnings, the chosen publisher's merits and demerits are bound to be closely examined. Does he market successfully? Does he keep his books in print? Does he own a paperback imprint? Is the publisher, whose personality stamps the image of the firm, backed up by a competent team who can provide continuity on his death or retirement? These are some of the questions an agent discusses with his author. No wonder some publishers are found wanting and blame the agent for the poverty of their list. It is seldom you will find the successful publisher or author writing to *The Times* to complain about the financial inadequacies of the book trade.

So what are the qualifications needed by an individual who sets out to protect and exploit the special interests of the author? Let me leave it to Heinemann again to put it in a nutshell: 'The literary agent is a favourite resort of persons who have not ability enough for ordinary business pursuits or for literature.'

Well, yes. And publishing . . . ? The fact is that publishers and agents are, to a degree, looking at each other across the same fence. The similarities of the two trades are greater than their differences. Many agents these days have served some time as publishers. The ability to appraise a manuscript, to judge its potential, to give editorial advice if needed, and if required, are qualities common to both the publisher and the agent. In a good relationship which, in recent years since the growing professionalism of agents, is increasingly common, the interests of the author, the agent and the publisher are seen to be nearly identical. Almost gone are the days when an agent felt it was wise to keep an author at arm's length from his publisher. Beginning to disappear, although still too frequently in evidence, is the myopic publisher who tries to persuade an author to leave his agent. What is now more commonly accepted is that all three have parts to play, none of which should conflict with the interests of the others. An agent's job is to help his author – if the help is required –

editorially and in any other fashion where he can offer support – and then to co-operate as closely as possible with the publisher to see that the book is published, promoted and sold to the general benefit of all three. Some evidence of the change in attitude, since the days of Heinemann, is witnessed by the fact that many publishers actively prefer agented manuscripts knowing that they are pre-selected, for no agent can afford to take on and submit a manuscript unless he regards the publishing prospects as good. Publishers, therefore, take agented submissions more seriously than the unsolicited manuscripts which continue to pour sadly through the post, yellowed and grimy with age as they wander hopelessly from destination to destination. They also find that it is simpler to negotiate with an agent over the details of a contract, leaving it to him to explain to the author the technical problems of the bargain. It is probably true that most publishers now consider that the professional agents – at least those who know their job – have an effective and necessary part to play in the increasingly complex business of publishing and selling books. Of course every agent is familiar with the slightly contemptuous and patronizing holier-than-thou attitude which he encounters from time to time, both from author and publisher. I accept it with only a degree of irritation from an author whose creative spark enables the rest of the book trade to exist. I refuse to accept it from a publisher who seems to imagine that an investment of money, rarely nowadays his own, gives him a social, intellectual and financial edge which is so frequently and laughably discounted by the pathetic results he achieves. So, though it would be an exaggeration to state that agents have come to be loved (except, now and then, by their authors), perhaps, like the tax man, the trade now gives them grudging acceptance.

For myself, I can merely be thankful that my professional life has given me more fun, more rewarding friendships (though possibly less money) than I could have expected in any other occupation, including that of publishing. Looking back I would not have wanted any of it to have been different.

INDEX